I0626435

Orange Crush

ENDORSEMENTS

"I definitely endorse this book, it not only depicts my time with the Astros but it's a true account of my time with them, I hope people can laugh, smile, or frown, enjoy."

- **Scipio Spinks**, Former ML pitcher

"Thinking about "what if" is one of the most fun aspects of sports. What if that trade hadn't been made? What if this player had been a starter instead of that player? Samuel Barrett has written an excellent book about what ifs concerning the 1971 Houston Astros. But he doesn't just speculate as if he were among a bunch of guys reminiscing. He uses statistics and expert analysis to show how a team that was sub-.500 could have gone all the way. Barrett is a true baseball aficionado, and *The Neglected 1971 Houston Astros: Orange Crush* is an excellent and worthy successor to his previous baseball book, *Umpire Diary*."

- **William S. Bike**, author of *The Forgotten 1970 Chicago Cubs: Go and Glow, Streets of the Near West Side,* and *Winning Political Campaigns*

"The 1971 Houston Astros were a fascinating team—quirky, gritty, and full of stories that didn't always make the headlines... The Astros played 75 one-run games in 1971, which remains an all-time MLB record. J.R. Richard's electric debut on September 5, 1971, 15 strikeouts, tying Karl Spooner's record for most strikeouts in a debut game. Joe Morgan's final season with Houston before being traded to Cincinnati, where he'd become a two-time MVP, in the infamous deal that helped build the Big Red Machine. We only skimmed the surface, but Samuel Barrett dives deep—unearthing the untold stories and hidden details that bring the history of the '71 Astros, and several additional Houston rosters, to life in bold, brilliant strokes."

- **Sean Holtz** CEO / Founder, Baseball Almanac, Inc.

"No expansion franchise ever amassed such terrific young talent as quickly as Houston, and none managed to give away as many key pieces. By 1971, the ball club was left with a handful of real stars and a bundle of what ifs. Samuel Barrett's examination of this team is a long overdue look at a fascinating moment of baseball history."

- **Mike Vance**, author of *Houston Baseball: The Early Years*

"The Houston Astros of the late 1960s and early 1970s did not win any championships or pennants, nor did they even win a division title. But the Houston franchise of that era provides a fascinating study in missteps, mistakes, and tragedies, as laid out in rich detail by Samuel Barrett in his new book. No longer a downtrodden expansion franchise by 1971, the Colt .45s-turned-Astros featured a thriving farm system that was producing enough talent to win the National League West. With young stars like Joe Morgan, Bob Watson, Cesar Cedeno, Jimmy Wynn, and Don Wilson, those Astros should have won more games in a division that was primed for the taking. But as Barrett explains in his comprehensive storyline, the franchise made too many unwise trades and lacked the leadership needed to win. It was a blueprint for how not to take that next step from contender to championship team – and Barrett lays it all out with an enjoyable and insightful narrative."

- **Bruce Markusen**, author of *The Team That Changed Baseball: Roberto Clemente and the 1971 Pittsburgh Pirates*

ORANGE CRUSH

THE NEGLECTED
1971 HOUSTON ASTROS

SAMUEL BARRETT

Published by Huntsville Independent Press

2112 Morningside Drive NW, Huntsville, AL, 35810

ORANGE CRUSH: The Neglected 1971 Houston Astros is a work of creative nonfiction based on the author's research and perspectives gained via that research. Names and details may have been altered for privacy. The opinions expressed are those of the author and do not necessarily reflect the views of the publisher.

Huntsville Independent Press can bring authors to your live event. For more information or to book an event, contact Huntsville Independent Press at +1 (256) 678-0411 or visit our website at www.HuntsvilleIndependent.com.

Cover design by Chris Treccani - 3 Dog Creative
Interior design by Chris Treccani - 3 Dog Creative

The text for this book was set in Adobe Garamond Pro.

Manufactured in the United States of America
First HIP paperback edition September 2025

12345678910

The Library of Congress has cataloged the hardcover edition as follows:

Names: Samuel Barrett, author.

Title: Orange Crush

LCCN (Pending)
Identifiers: ISBN 979-8-9927321-4-6 (paperback)
979-8-9927321-5-3 (hardcover)
979-8-9927321-3-9 (ebook)

CONTENTS

FOREWORD
BY JOE THOMPSON

I have always had a simple message when it comes to talking about baseball. Everyone, no matter who they are, loves to talk about a game they played growing up. For many people, one of the games they played was baseball. And when you talk to anyone who played baseball at some point of their lives, I have found that pretty much everyone has a baseball story to tell. Whether that story is about something they did on the field or a story about their favorite players or teams, stories about baseball are everywhere and people, whether they know it or not, love to talk about baseball stories or hear a good baseball story. This is why I joined SABR in 2010 and why I have preached the message of baseball and its many stories to countless people primarily in the Houston area and everywhere else I go.

In January 2024, Samuel sent me a message on LinkedIn about wanting to have a chance to speak with the Larry Dierker Houston SABR chapter about something Astros-history related that he was working on. As the Houston SABR chapter President, I am always looking for different people to share their work on baseball, no matter what the subject material. He told me that he had been doing research on the Astros teams of the 1960s and early 1970s. When I heard this, I asked him if he could share his research with our group. We worked out a schedule date for his talk about his time as an umpire and his book about one particular season. Just before he was scheduled to talk with us, he told me about his project on the 1971 Astros. As a lifelong Astros fan, I was curious to hear what he would say about that team. He then told me that the 1971 team could have been something special if things had worked out.

I met JR Richard a few years before he passed away at an Astros Fan Fest event. JR was one of my favorite players because my earlier memory of attending an Astros game involved him. My Dad worked at the Astrodome and there was a time when my Mom, little brother, and I could sit in the left field seats and watch the game while my Dad finished up his job for the night. My earliest memory of attending a game happened on a day when JR was pitching and we were waiting for my Dad. I do not know all the details but what has permanently burned in my memory is that he struck out over ten batters and everyone around me was talking about how great this guy was. I looked on this field and even though we were a long way away from the pitching mound, I always thought JR looked like a giant who could do what he wanted to any batter he faced. I told JR this story when I met him and I could tell what this meant to him. Here was someone who had been through so much in his life being reminded again why people loved him so much.

My first Astros hero, JR Richard, made his debut with the club in 1971. Samuel makes the point in this book that the 1971 team could have been something special. That makes for a story that a lot of Astros and baseball fans have probably never heard before. To circle back to my original point, this is why baseball stories are great. You never know what you are going to hear about when someone tells you a baseball story.

In closing, I can give you one absolute truth about my first baseball memory. I did not attend JR Richard's debut on September 5, 1971. My dad did not work at the Astrodome then, and I was only eighteen days old.

Joseph L. Thompson, Ph.D.
President, Larry Dierker Chapter, Houston, TX,
Society of American Baseball Research (SABR)
Faculty Lecturer, C.T. Bauer College of Business,
University of Houston

ACKNOWLEDGEMENTS

Writing a book with this much detail about a year that was twenty-nine years before I was born in 2000, and fifty-three years before 2024 when I wrote the rough draft, was a trying experience, but one that I found great resources for and enjoyed the process of. Given my young age and the amount of time that has passed since 1971, I knew that I could not do this alone, though I did not desire to, either. Therefore, there are many people who contributed to this project in a variety of ways, so I say about this acknowledgements section the same thing President Abraham Lincoln said in his Gettysburg Address: "It is altogether fitting and proper that [I] should do this."

Biologically, no person becomes anything without their parents. I am no exception, and my parents have never given up on me, even when it probably would have been easy for them to accept less for me. When I was first diagnosed with autism spectrum disorder when I was young, the doctors told my mother that I would never speak to her. No mother wants to hear such a limiting blanket statement about what their own child will be incapable of, and mine decided that what she heard was not good enough. Our access to excellent early intervention in Decatur Alabama helped me to eventually speak to her. The doctors qualified their previous statement by saying that she would be the only person I would ever speak to. Of course today, you can see that that did not last, either. However, the condition that I would still never be able to operate in a standard classroom setting was still maintained by the experts, who were certain that I would need to enroll in special education classes. I imagine my mother was full of questions: Would I ever move out on my own? Would I ever be able to drive a car? Would I ever hold down a job? Would I even be able to make friends? Those have only begun to be disproven in recent years, but the chips were well in place early in my life to make sure that I could do these things, and that is because of the endless love and perseverance by my family, at a time when I was incapable of those feelings for myself. Only a truly selfless soul would be willing to shift their attention away from themselves and toward someone else to such a degree that my parents did. My parents certainly are not the only people that have ever made such sacrifices, but at least among the friends I gained during and since high school, I'd bet that none of their parents had to do so to the degree that mine had to just to get me to the point where I could start kindergarten on time with my sister Anna Grace and other peers our age. The massive efforts made by my family surely have made my academic achievements, social interactions, and outgoing endeavors such as going to umpire school and writing books, very rewarding in my family's eyes.

Just as my immediate family made sacrifices and efforts for me, my grandparents have shown me an equal amount of love. I have two grandparents on my father's side who live in Suwanee, Georgia, and look for any opportunity to do for their children and grandchildren. They are originally from south Texas, with my father being born in San Antonio in 1966 and their family living in Texas City for the first decade of my father's life until 1975. This means that they lived close to Houston during the time period of the Astros I write about in this book, but unfortunately, they were not interested much in the Astros during that time, so they could not provide recollections from watching the team. Still, it is because of them and their heritage that I came to watch the Astros in the first place, which eventually led to the production of this book.

On my mother's side, my grandfather has been my most relatable relative, and my Nana, who is not biologically related to me and my sister but nonetheless still claim us as her grandchildren, enjoys showing her love whenever she can. My biological maternal grandmother died in October of 2009, but that was not before my sister and I got to know her well enough to look forward to seeing her whenever we could.

The layout of this book is based largely off of the book *The Forgotten 1970 Chicago Cubs: Go and Glow*, by William Bike. Bike argues that the 1970 Cubs were better than the famous 1969 team (As do many others, including myself) and breaks down the season and the potential postseason games in a way that I felt would be effective to emulate. I got in touch with Bike early in 2024, and he has been enthusiastic to help in any way he could. He even said that he would be honored if I based my book off his, so I hope he will be honored by the fact that this idea now exists as a print book.

On the same day that I talked to Bike for the first time, I also had an informative phone call with Houston-area author Mike Vance. He, along with many others whom I will thank a little later, provided great insights and facts about the period of the Astros I was researching. Whether it be about the roster development and evolution, the front office composition, the Astrodome, or other fine details, Vance was able to help, and he also gave me some good insights on writing and being an author, as he has become many times.

Bike and Vance both suggested reaching out to the Society for American Baseball Research (SABR), specifically the appropriately named Larry Dierker SABR Chapter in Houston, so I did. Chapter President Joe Thompson and member Mike McCroskey, among others, were great in helping get the word out about the production of this book and referring me to others who could help.

The most exhilarating part of researching and writing this book was speaking with folks who were part of the team during the late-60's and early-70's, particularly in 1971. Former front office executive Tal Smith, the team's ace pitcher Larry Dierker (Both of whom are also SABR members), outfielder Norm Miller, relief pitcher George Culver, starting/relief pitcher Tom Griffin, pitcher Scipio Spinks, and pitcher Larry Yount were great to talk with and listen to.

As for the current Astros, their Senior Vice President, Marketing and Communications Anita Sehgal and Broadcast Manager Ginny Grande helped out in the production of this project as well. I was able to reach out to several of the former players and team members listed above via the Astros organization's helping hand.

Ben Gibson of The History Press returned a query I sent through the Arcadia Publishing website to begin conversation about this book, and he was both friendly and substantive in his advice as I prepared my writing for proposal.

Joshua Adams of Huntsville Independent Press is very clearly passionate and dedicated to his craft for writing and publishing, and he exemplified that to me through his assistance of looking over my writing and giving me advice on how to overcome obstacles that came up while pursuing publication of the book you are now holding. He is the one who ultimately believed in me and my writing enough to accept this book for publication through HIP, and I see now that my patience was more than rewarded with the perfect home for my work.

Sean Holtz of Baseball-Almanac.com has done a phenomenal job of putting together one of the most comprehensive baseball sources on the internet today, and I still refer to that website whenever I need a tidbit of information that I do not have. He has also corresponded with me for several years now, so his help and platform have been great as well.

Newspapers.com was a gold mine for game breakdowns and articles written back in 1971, as well as other photos taken and published in newspapers back then. To all the writers of the articles and papers in which I cite, and the photographers whose photos are included within these pages, I thank you incredibly.

The last acknowledgement goes to the Almighty. The Lord our God has provided all these people, opened the opportunities to write and publish this book, and has long since gotten me to a point where I would be capable of considering putting together a project such as a book. When I pray to Him for the life He can give to me, I tell him the same thing Steve Harvey says he prayed when he was homeless: if you let me get there, I'll tell everybody it was You. Well, here I am, and it was God. Sure, you can write a book without Him, but chances are those who say that are either not writing a book or not getting through the things that He carried me through.

To anyone whom I have neglected to mention, I promise it is not on purpose, and you are greatly appreciated as well.

INTRODUCTION

Houston Texas, after years of Buffs minor league baseball, attempts to lure existing MLB franchises such as the St. Louis Browns and Cardinals and the Cleveland Indians, and consideration for a charter Continental League franchise, received a Major League Baseball team in 1961. After completing an expansion draft alongside the other National League expansion team, the New York Mets, the Houston Colt 45s began play in 1962. In 1965, the team was renamed the Astros due to trademark issues and owner Judge Roy Hofheinz chose to adopt a new identity rather than share profits. From that point, many revolutionary aspects of baseball originated deep in the heart of Texas. From the first indoor ballpark to the first artificial playing surface to the first primarily-orange color scheme, the traditionally steadfast game of baseball was not exempt from the beginnings of counterculture, and the Space City fielded one of the most active teams in baseball in that regard.

The on-field success of the Astros during the team's first decade is not often remembered, partially because there was not much of it. The team did not reach the .500 mark for a season until 1969 and did not finish with a winning record until 1972, and even both of those records could be considered underperformances given the findings you will discover in this book. In the first few years of the franchise's operations, the scouting and development department for the ballclub, led by farm system director Tal Smith, signed a plethora of talented young prospects who went on to have distinguished Major League careers. Unfortunately, second baseman Joe Morgan, one of those prospects, was correct when he said in his autobiography *Joe Morgan: A Life in Baseball* that "It turned out that there were reasons for it [Not winning], beyond the simple facts of youth and inexperience."[1] A shift in personnel at the top led to a shift in personnel on the field, which, partnered with a less-than-first-class experience for the latter, resulted in no shift in the team's performance on the field.

At first glance, it is easy to blame the team's lack of competitiveness on it being an expansion franchise still adapting to big league operations. However, given how well many of the team's young players performed, whether it be in Houston or after they were shipped off elsewhere, it is easy to see how the Astros missed out on better seasons and postseason opportunities. At the same time, their expansion mate Mets had come around and won the World Series in 1969, albeit with a subpar lineup on paper that warranted that season being considered a miracle run, hence the nickname "Miracle Mets." Surely an Astros team with a more fortified roster and better leadership than the Mets would have made a dent in the National League postseason discussions more than they did. Would they have out-slugged the weak-hitting Los Angeles Dodgers? Brought more color than the Big Red Machine Cincinnati Reds? Made smaller the aspirations of the San Francisco Giants? Scared the Atlanta Braves? Took the coveted National League pennant from the St. Louis Cardinals, Chicago Cubs, New York Mets, and Pittsburgh Pirates? Held off the Baltimore Orioles, Detroit Tigers, Oakland A's, Boston Red Sox, and Minnesota Twins to reach baseball's pinnacle by bringing a World Series title to Houston?

The 1971 Houston Astros, like the Astros' teams of previous seasons, was a ballclub full of young talent who had developed into big league stars, and a few who were still developing. Some of the homegrown players who began to make their names in Houston were "Bull" Bob Watson at first base, future National Baseball Hall of Famer Joe Morgan at second base, and the "Red Rooster" Doug Rader at third base. Denis Menke and Roger Metzger, transplants from the Braves and Cubs organizations, respectively, held the position of shortstop. In the AstroTurf outfield, Jimmy Wynn had made a name for himself as the "Toy Cannon," as he was one of few players able to clear the wall at the Astrodome, as well as hit monster home runs away from Houston, and he stood only 5'9" and weighed 165 lbs. In June 1970, center fielder Cesar Cedeno came up and began to light up the baseball world with his effortless elite ability that quickly earned him a spot in the starting lineup. Watson also played left field, and guys like Norm Miller, Jesus Alou, and Cesar Geronimo filled the rest of the pasture. Veteran pennant-winning catcher Johnny Edwards was the starting catcher, and he was known for his defense and his ability to motivate pitchers. Jack Hiatt and homegrown Larry Howard backed him up without sacrificing skill on Edwards' rest days.

The Astros' pitching was just as full of homegrown saplings. Larry Dierker was the ace, having become the first Houston pitcher to win 20 games in 1969 and then winning 16 games in 1970. Don Wilson had two no-hitters to his credit as he used the strikeout effectively. Tom Griffin and Ken Forsch were each called up in 1969 and 1970, respectively, and each began their careers well. Jim Ray was a mainstay in the bullpen, as were transplants George Culver and closer Fred Gladding. Young prospects Buddy Harris, Bill Greif, and Scipio Spinks competed for roles throughout the season.

As vibrant as the Astros' skill was, the team was still not excelling at the level many fans in Houston believed they could, and it was the team's own front office that had made some poor decisions that led to a lack of competitiveness. In addition to the homegrown players that were with the team in 1971, the Astros had signed and developed the likes of solid-hitting right fielder Rusty Staub, workhorse pitcher Dave Giusti, athletic shortstop Sonny Jackson, and dependable catcher both at and behind the plate Jerry Grote. The ballclub had also acquired from other clubs guys like fan-favorite third baseman Bob Aspromonte, starting pitcher Mike Cuellar, reliable pinch-hitter and outfielder Manny Mota, future All Star second baseman Sandy Alomar, and fleetfooted defensive whiz in the outfield Cesar Geronimo. The stellar combination of home-signed youngsters and selective signing and trading with other teams created a future for the Astros as bright as the stars that real-life astronauts see when they go into space.

However, Paul Richards, with his cocky personality, did not remain the general manager to see the fruit of his labor, and when the hands of power changed, so did the approach to running the ballclub. The new general manager, H.B. "Spec" Richardson, prioritized immediate fanfare and success over development for the future, so he began to replace the young stars with veterans who were past the prime of their careers and he hired known racist and closed-minded coach Harry "The Hat" Walker to be the team's manager. Meanwhile, in the franchise's tenth season, the fans of Houston were waiting for a championship ballclub, especially after seeing the Mets, who had come into existence at the same time the Houston Colt 45s did, win it all in 1969.

This book will specifically cover the 1971 Astros season as that is the first likely season of what would have been an expected elite Astros team, but the reasons why this team was not a World Series contender date back to some disastrous front office decisions in the years prior to 1971, so the story of any Astros season from 1969 up until 1980, when the Astros finally made the postseason for the first time, cannot be told without examining these executive moves. Looking back, discerning fans can speculate how much better the team's performance would have been had the team's leadership stayed patient.

BACKGROUND

The first big story that stemmed from the Houston Astros was the opening of the first indoor ballpark, a dome christened the Astrodome once the team's name was chosen. With those franchise-characterizing milestones came a lot of the young players that would make up the core of the pennant-contending Astros later in the decade. The scouting department had been working hard to scout as many future stars who could run and play defense as they could since that was the type of player general manager Paul Richards desired, and going into 1965, the big league club had a lineup that reads like an All Star team: Second baseman Joe Morgan, third baseman Bob Aspromonte, center fielder Jimmy Wynn, and right fielder Rusty Staub were in the starting lineup, with shortstop Sonny Jackson getting a taste of the big leagues as well.[1] On the mound, Larry Dierker, Mike Cuellar, and Dave Giusti were beginning their big league seasoning. Catcher Jerry Grote and pitcher Joe Hoerner were also around, but only in Oklahoma City, and both were either traded or lost via draft after the season. The final record for the season was 65-97 and Joe Morgan finished second in National League Rookie of the Year voting behind the Dodgers' Jim Lefebvre, despite Morgan having better numbers in almost every offensive statistic, as the Astros' aesthetic impact on baseball was just beginning.

1

The Astrodome opened its doors to the Astros and to Houston in 1965 and quickly earned the appropriate title of "The Eighth Wonder of the World."

When discussing the reasons why the Astros from the late 60's to early 70's did not contend, the first domino to fall fell in 1965. R.E. "Bob" Smith, the team's majority owner, helped to fund the team and many of Judge Roy Hofheinz's big ideas. An ongoing rift between Smith and Hofheinz about decision-making, and especially about how much credit for the business was given to Hofheinz and not Smith, became enough to break apart the partnership. As an aside regarding this rift, it did not help when Hofheinz did not invite Smith to the skybox that U.S. President Lyndon B. Johnson was in during the opening exhibition game at the Dome until the seventh inning. They agreed a deal that would give one of them sole ownership of the franchise: Hofheinz was to give Smith $7.5 million by August 12 to buy out Smith's share of the team. If, by that date, Hofheinz could not pay that sum, Smith would pay and buy out Hofheinz. The deal was announced on May 13, by which time Smith had agreed to it, believing that Hofheinz would not be able to come up with the money, or at least not in time. He did, however, and on August 2, Smith was out of the picture of Houston baseball.[2]

Once Bob Smith was bought out, Hofheinz wasted little time making his own moves. He fired general manager Paul Richards after Richards did not allow Hofheinz to be involved with roster decisions. Looking back at how things turned out, Hofheinz would have been better off leaving the baseball moves to others involved such as Richards and farm system director Tal Smith as they were more knowledgeable with the baseball side of the business than Hofheinz was. But the deed was done, and the 1966 Astros front office was run by a group of three people: Tal Smith, new field manager Grady Hatton, and business administrator H.B. "Spec" Richardson.

Adaptation in the baseball realm was already underway in Houston as the team faced the distinction of playing home games under a roof, so they might as well take on anything else that would be necessitated by the new playing conditions. That's what the Astros got in 1966. When Joe Morgan first saw the Astrodome, his first thought was that glare coming from the translucent roof during day games would be a problem. The media criticized Morgan for doubting architects, but he soon proved to be right, as during the 1965 season, easy fly balls for Major League players were not caught.[3] Pitcher Larry Dierker expressed concern that he would be demoted to the minor leagues because his outfield was not making outs. The roof was painted to help the players see the ball better, but the natural Bermuda grass began to die, despite that breed of grass being chosen because of its ability to grow in less-than-ideal circumstances. Judge Hofheinz assigned the task of finding a solution to Tal Smith, who found one in the northeast U.S. An artificial grass surface to replace the Bermuda grass was acquired and installed in the infield–Monsanto would provide the outfield materials later in the summer. Judge Hofheinz, the same marketing genius that named the domed stadium the "Astrodome" gave the new playing surface a similar name: AstroTurf. The Astros now had to adjust to quicker hits and bounces off the hyperactive turf or else they would either get hit in the mouth, demoted to the minors, or both.

The new grass was not the only change the Astros faced for the 1966 season. When Hofheinz let Richards go, he also had an assistant fire manager Luman Harris over the phone, since Harris was considered one of Richards' "yes men." After the triple-A affiliate Oklahoma City 89ers' manager Grady Hatton proved his loyalty to the Astros' franchise by not accepting the job managing the Chicago White Sox, he was promoted to be the big league manager in Houston.[4]

Several of the players on the Astros were excited about Hatton coming up to the big leagues with them since they remembered playing under him in Triple-A and winning two Pacific Coast League championships.[5] Hatton was also definitely a Texan, having played college baseball at the University of Texas in Austin and played in the big leagues for the Reds, White Sox, Red Sox, Cardinals, Orioles, and Cubs.[6] He began managing with the Houston Buffs and stayed with them until 1961 when he joined the Colt 45s organization, under which he managed the triple-A Oklahoma City 89ers. His OKC teams, with future Orange Crush Astros on them, won Pacific Coast League pennants in 1963 and 1965. Hatton took the reins of the Astros in 1966 and instilled discipline and organization (Which is possibly why he wore uniform number 1 and the rest of the coaching staff also wore single-digit numbers). They believed that it wouldn't be too long before they replicated that result at the Major League level.

After leading the triple-A Oklahoma City 89ers to two Pacific Coast League pennants, Grady Hatton was rewarded with the skipper position with the Major League club in 1966.

These two new advantages in the Astros' favor did not lead to immediate success as they began the season on the wrong side of the win/loss column, but it didn't take too long for the tide to turn as they landed themselves in second place in the National League on May 11. They did not just float there for a day either - they maintained that position for a little over two weeks, and remained in third place for six days leading up to that ascent and for eight days after they dropped to that spot, which carried the schedule into June.[7]

That was the high point of the season for the Astros, and as with any team, especially one that is still trying to develop, there were some low points as well. On July 25, the team lost the first game of a Dome series against the Mets, dropping the Astros record below .500 for the first time since April 29. On the first day of August in Philadelphia, center fielder Jimmy Wynn collided with the outfield wall at Shibe Park/Connie Mack Stadium and broke his left elbow, wrist, and hand, ending his season.[8]

The team's final line was an improvement over 1965 with a 72-90 record, which settled them into eighth place. When Wynn was forced off the field due to injury, he had already hit 18 home runs and knocked in 62 runs. Third baseman Bob Aspromonte did not have an extraordinary year, but he was keeping his designation as Aspro the Astro as he knocked 8 home runs, all but one in August, including one each in the first three consecutive games that month. He also maintained a solid .252 batting average. Right fielder Rusty Staub provided 13 long balls and 81 runs batted in. The season after second baseman Joe Morgan's breakout, the shortstop position fostered its guy. Sonny Jackson finished second in NL Rookie of the Year voting, just as Morgan had done in 1965, by stealing 49 bases and leading the Astros by batting .292, supplementing Morgan's own .285 clip and All Star team spot. Tommy Helms of the Cincinnati Reds won the ROY award, even though Jackson's stats were better. This means the Astros's keystone sack combination was wrongfully kept from baseball honors two seasons in a row.

Morgan was supposed to be the National League's starting second baseman in the Midsummer Classic, but he did not play due to a broken kneecap. Morgan and Jackson began to grow together, and the media caught onto what they viewed as possibly the best double play combination in the National League for years to come. Photoshoots and an appearance on the cover of Sports Illustrated, the first by an Astros player, punctuated this belief in the up-and-coming keystone core.[9] Pitcher Dave Giusti also made his name known by winning 15 games, including a one-hit shutout in San Francisco and another shutout in a game in which he drove in six runs, the majority of the Astros' runs, in an 11-0 clouting of the Reds. Mike Cuellar also headlined the Astros' pitching when he fell short of only the legendary Sandy Koufax in league ERA when he put up a 2.22. Koufax somehow topped that with a 1.73 to win his third pitching Triple Crown. Cuellar also added 12 wins of his own, and Larry Dierker supplied 10 more and a 3.18 ERA. The team had a winning record at home, going 45-36 for the third time in franchise history and the first time as the Astros, and they also finished the first half of the season over .500, playing 45-40 ball. They had winning records against the Cubs, Reds, and Cardinals.

There was a great deal of optimism around the Astros going into 1967, which was evident by the team having the third-highest attendance in baseball the year before as 1,872,108 spectators entered the Astrodome for baseball. On New Year's Eve of 1966, the Astros traded a couple of pitchers to the Atlanta Braves for two names that could ring large with the Astros: middle infielder Sandy Alomar and legendary third baseman Eddie Mathews. Alomar later became an All Star second baseman with the Angels,

Second baseman Joe Morgan quickly matured into both a table setter and defensive asset for the young Astros, earning a Rookie of the Year nomination and All Star nod in his first two full big league seasons.

and Mathews bridged the gap between Bob Aspromonte and Doug Rader at third base. He also filled in at first base before being traded to Detroit on August 17 in exchange for closing pitcher Fred Gladding. Mathews would also be a strong mentor for the young ballclub during his four-and-a-half months in Houston, during which he hit his 500th career home run.

Another move during the 1967 season came in the front office, when the three-man general management experiment was jettisoned, and Spec Richardson was promoted to be the full-time general manager on July 27 as a reward from Hofheinz for being loyal to him and doing anything Hofheinz asked, even if it was against Hofheinz's doctor's orders.[10] This simple shift in leadership would be more detrimental to the potential of the Astros than anything else.

The team's record fell in 1967, but individually, several of the Astros' young stars had big seasons. At the start of the season, the Astros had Joe Morgan at second base, Bob Aspromonte at third, Sonny Jackson at shortstop, Jimmy Wynn in center field, and Rusty Staub in right as the guys in the batting lineup who would have become part of an "Orange Crush" championship team. On the mound, Larry Dierker, Mike Cuellar, Dave Giusti, and Don Wilson had made their way to The Show by this point. For the season, Mike Cuellar won 16 games, becoming the first Houston pitcher to do so. Jimmy Wynn hit 37 home runs and nearly led the National League in long balls. Rusty Staub compiled a .333 batting average, a franchise record, to combine with Wynn and solidify center field and right field, respectively. All three of them were awarded for their excellence with All Star Game selections, making the 1967 Midsummer Classic the first one with multiple Astros.[11] At Anaheim Stadium, the site of the All Star Game, both Wynn and Staub collected singles, while Cuellar pitched two scoreless innings, with a single by the Red Sox' Carl Yastrzemski being his only flaw.[12]

Starting pitcher Mike Cuellar bounced around the Reds and Cardinals organizations before beginning his ascent in Houston, where Grady Hatton said he had "created a monster" out of Cuellar.

When it comes to Jimmy Wynn's power numbers in 1967, those deserve some attention all on their own. In addition to his franchise-record 37 home runs, he drove in 107 runs, becoming the first Houston player to reach 35 homers and 100 RBI in one season, and had a slugging percentage of .495. He battled the Braves' Henry Aaron all season long for the league lead in home runs, but Aaron ultimately won out by two when Wynn finished the season with sixteen straight games without a homer. Wynn also fell just short of the NL RBI title when Orlando Cepeda finished with 111. Still, Wynn's powerful drives still resonate with fans today due to his comparatively small frame for a baseball player at 5'9" and 165 lbs.

Two of his 37 homers in '67 are still easy to find online. On June 11 in his hometown of Cincinnati, he barely felt a Sammy Ellis pitch touch his bat as he launched the ball over the Crosley Field scoreboard and onto the interstate, then bounding into a neighborhood and onto the street in which he grew up.[13] July 23 in Pittsburgh provided another chance to take the breath away from the fans, as Wynn did when he muscled a ball over the fence in straightaway center field, which at Forbes Field, was 457 feet from home plate.[14] It was so far that, if you see the clip of that home run online, you'll see that the Pirates grounds grew would store the batting cage by the center field fence because they figured no one would reach it. Wynn wrote that the ball found a Little League field behind Forbes Field. A lesser-known power performance by the Toy Cannon came on June 15 when he knocked three balls over the Astrodome fence against the Giants, including two off starter Bobby Bolin, in a 6-2 Mike Cuellar win. These shows of power prompted Houston Chronicle writer John Wilson to tab Wynn as the "Toy Cannon." The nickname Toy Cannon stuck from then on.

On June 18, Father's Day, Don Wilson, who had just been called up the previous September, threw a no-hitter under the Dome against the Atlanta Braves, after which Braves slugger Henry Aaron said, "It's young guys like this that make me want to retire."

Bob Watson got a cup of coffee in September, playing in six games, including a game in Pittsburgh on the last day of the month in which he crushed his first Major League home run, which brought his batting average up to .200. That home run made the difference for his team in a 4-3 win over the Pirates. The day before, Watson was at first base as he started his first big league game, and he ended up there again when he collected his first hit.[15] Half a month before Eddie Mathews was traded away, the Astros called up Doug Rader, a young infielder to learn from the future Hall of Famer and supplement Bob Aspromonte.

In the American League in 1967, there was a young ballclub that rose up to perform very well under a manager who, like Astros manager Grady Hatton, had managed several of the now-big league players when they were in Triple-A, and who was well-liked by many. That manager being Dick Williams of the Boston Red Sox. So, as the Astros watched the World Series during their offseason, it's very possible that many members of the team saw what the Red Sox had done in a circumstance like what they themselves now had, and got inspiration from that, sparking what would have been another great season in 1968.

Jimmy Wynn's hometown home run over Crosley Field scoreboard. June 11, 1967

Jimmy Wynn's dead-center shot over batting cage at Forbes Field. July 23, 1967

The start of the 1968 season was delayed in the aftermath of the MLK Jr. assassination, only the first of several off-the-field stories that would captivate the United States in 1968.[16] When the season did get underway, despite the Astros having traded Sonny Jackson to the Braves, the Astros got off to their best start in franchise history with a record of 5-1. Larry Dierker won his first career Opening Day start against the Pirates when Bob Aspromonte walked off the Pirates. The team's first loss was at home against the Mets on April 14, but a bigger blow to the Astros occurred during that game: Joe Morgan was injured when Tommie Agee performed a takeout slide to break up a double play, and the Houston second baseman was out for the season. However, this allowed him to still attend every home game and learn from watching the games this year. He taught himself the idiosyncrasies of the Astrodome and what to watch on each pitcher to get a better jump off them when attempting to steal bases. This self-education was common for Morgan, as during his rookie season of 1965, he quickly picked up the quirks of each ballpark and learned how to face tough pitchers.[17]

The day after that on April 15, the Astros collected their fifth win, which marked three straight days that the Astros were in sole possession of first place in the National League. The Mets' Tom Seaver and the Astros' Don Wilson started that game that went 24 innings and lasted over six hours. In the top of the twentieth inning, the AstroLite scoreboard displayed a message that read, "WE HOPE YOU'RE ENJOYING TONIGHT'S THIRD GAME AS MUCH AS YOU DID THE FIRST TWO."[18] Mercifully, in the bottom of the twenty-fourth inning, Astros' third baseman Bob Aspromonte hit a ground ball that rolled between Mets' shortstop Al Weis's legs, allowing Norm Miller to score the winning—and only—run of the night. The Astros won 1-0.[19]

1968 was certainly an eventful year for the Astros as much as it was for all of baseball and the country. Willie Mays celebrated his thirty-seventh birthday on May 6 during a Giants' trip to Houston with a large 569-pound cake (One pound for each of his home runs at the time) from Judge Roy Hofheinz and a 10-2 loss to the Astros in which Rusty Staub went 4-for-4 with a 2 RBI double and 6 total RBI on the day.[20] Owner Judge Hofheinz opened AstroWorld on June 1, though the Astros lost in the Dome that day to the Cubs 3-1.[21] At the same time, the National League announced that it was in the middle of the tightest race ever at that point in the season, with the Pirates, who were in last place, only five games behind the first place San Francisco Giants. The Astros were in eighth place and merely four games behind. However, the pipe dream of pennant fever would not last in H-Town.

*Legendary Willie Mays had an interesting 37ᵗʰ birthday,
with his team losing to the Astros in the Dome but being given
a large birthday cake pregame.*

Also in May, the National League announced that it would expand to field two new teams in San Diego California and Montreal Quebec in Canada. There were several cities vying for one of these coveted franchises either in the National or American League, and one of the markets that applied for a NL team was Dallas-Fort Worth, as they felt that since Houston was succeeding, that they could too. When they were not awarded a ballclub, that area took great offense at being snubbed when they had a large market, especially being left out in favor of putting a team outside the country. Dallas-Fort Worth decided that the Astros, namely Judge Hofheinz, had something to do with the snub. Either he must have not worked hard enough to promote the neighboring market, or he worked hard to prevent competition in the same state. A Dallas newspaper published a photo of Hofheinz with a bullseye over it, a move that looking back, considering that it was not quite five years earlier that President John F. Kennedy was assassinated in Dallas, was not in good taste.[22] Houston fans still use this insensitivity as an example of Dallas's inferiority to the Space City.

Presidential candidate Robert F. Kennedy was assassinated on June 6, and his funeral was held on June 9. On that day, Bob Aspromonte, Rusty Staub, and Dave Giusti elected to sit out and not play in honor of the former president's brother, despite pressure from the Astros' front office not to do so. All three were traded during the following offseason.[23]

After a loss on June 17, Houston management decided that they had seen enough of Grady Hatton managing the ballclub, so he was dismissed and replaced with former Cardinals outfielder and Pirates manager Harry Walker, and the team began to win more games. Jimmy Wynn argues, however, that those wins came out of spite, as Walker began to fester a toxic, racist, and bigoted personality over the young and promising clubhouse.[24] He would disparage black players any chance he got, force his batting style and bat model onto hitters, and judge his guys' talent and viability on the Astros ballclub by their race and their loyalty to him more than their skill. Several of the poor trades that the Astros made leading up to 1971 were motivated by Walker's negative opinion of the players that the front office shipped away.

The All Star Game was hosted at the Astrodome, and Rusty Staub, the Astros' lone representative, popped out to third base against Denny McLain in a sixth inning pinch-hit appearance for Steve Carlton. The National League won their sixth straight Midsummer Classic with a 1-0 score.

The Astrodome in Houston hosted the MLB All Star Game in 1968, which exemplified the "Year of the Pitcher" that season when the game saw only one run scored.

Doug Rader sought and achieved retaliation against the Mets for injuring Joe Morgan when on August 7 in Houston, he slid into third base with his elbow up, injuring Kevin Collins.[25] A violent brawl ensued, but the Astros ultimately won 4-3.[26]

The final season record was 72-90, better than the previous season and the same as the season prior to that, but now they were in last place for the first time, even after starting the season in the best way they had up to that point. Before the 1968 season, whether it be in years prior or months prior, the organization had let go of catcher Jerry Grote, shortstop Sonny Jackson, and infielder Sandy Alomar. After the season, that is when a lot more broke down. Bad trades, poor evaluation of players, front office incompetency… everything wrong that the front office shakeups of 1965 caused or foreshadowed now came into the picture in the offseason of 1968-1969.

Going into 1969, expansion had thinned out the talent league-wide, but it had also introduced divisions, shrinking the number of teams the Astros had to compete against from nine in the whole league, to just five in the new National League West division. In addition, rules changes were introduced that were designed to help hitters after the "Year of the Pitcher" of 1968 was so detrimental to their success. The mound was low-ered by five inches, and the strike zone was shrunk, with the top lowering from the shoulders to the armpits.

The thinning of talent that most hurt the Astros was done by their own GM, Spec Richardson. Prospect first baseman Nate Colbert was left unprotected in the expansion draft, and Dave Giusti, Bob Aspromonte, Mike Cuellar, and Rusty Staub were all shipped away within four months. While the Astros did get veteran catcher Johnny Edwards and young pitcher Jack Billingham in two of those deals, the rest of the return was filled with guys who were past their primes or otherwise not worth what Richardson gave up. Common sense would dictate that if a team were willing to part with a veteran player, that veteran is past his prime and is no longer at the level he once was. This, along with subpar amenities in Spring Training at Cocoa Beach (Including midnight curfews), the con-tinued presence of Harry Walker, curfews during the regular season as well (Though they were dropped in 1971), and even the fact that Judge Hofheinz took in all of the money and made the players write checks for the cash rather than give out paychecks (So as to collect interest from the players' pay), resulted in a pessimistic, second-class culture to begin the season that was not helped when the team was swept in San Diego in the Padres' first-ever series, during which the Astros scored one run.[27] They came home to Houston and lost two more games to the Dodgers before winning their first game of the season.

At the end of April, the Astros had a 4-20 record and had just been no-hit by Jim Maloney of the Reds. May was much better, beginning with what is known as the "Revenge No-Hitter" by Don Wilson against the Reds the next day at Crosley Field, the second time ever that two pitchers on two opposing teams threw back-to-back no-hitters in the same park on consecutive days. No one had internalized the Astros' early-season frustra-tions more than Wilson, and coupled with the infuriating ways the Reds had taunted his team in earlier games, made for a determined Wilson as he arrived at the ballpark. Teammates quickly sensed this as their attempts to speak to him were not reciprocated, and after the final popout went from Tommy Helms' bat to Doug Rader's glove, the Astros swarmed Wilson, not just in celebration, but to keep him from reaching the Reds' dugout, where he was making his way towards. This exemplified Wilson's demeanor when provoked, which caused many blow-ups with manager Walker, but the game also proved to be an upward turning point for the ballclub.[28]

The rest of May saw the Astros set a record with seven double plays in one game, a ten-game winning streak (Which was replicated in June), and back-to-back walk off wins by Doug Rader. He hit a grand slam on May 25 and a single on the 26th, both in the bottom of the ninth on respective days. On June 11, Larry Dierker went the distance in an 11-inning game that ended with him knocking in the winning run on a single in the bottom of the eleventh.

As June turned to July, the Astros were trying to firmly grasp .500 as they had been going back and forth between .500 and just below it for the last few days. Shortstop Denis Menke, who was acquired in the exchange of Sonny Jackson, and Dierker made the All Star team as representatives of Houston. On July 20, the day of the Moon landing, the Astros were rained out in Cincinnati, but Judge Hofheinz most certainly would have devised a creative marketing promotion for that day had his team been at home.[29] Ten days later in New York, Denis Menke and Jimmy Wynn each hit a grand slam in the same inning in the first game of a doubleheader, and Larry Dierker hit a home run off of Nolan Ryan in the second game as the Astros took both ends of the twin bill.

Ball Four author Jim Bouton joined the team in late August, and he helped Houston go further into the pennant race than ever before, with the ballclub a mere two games behind first place on September 10. The National League even gave the Astros permission to print World Series tickets at this point. However, starting in mid-September, the rails fell off after a tough Larry Dierker loss in Atlanta three days later. On September 13, he carried a no-hitter into the ninth until Felix Millan broke it up with an infield single. Still, he kept pitching phenomenal ball, outlasting Phil Niekro by going twelve innings when Niekro only lasted eleven. John Mayberry pinch-hit for Dierker in the top of the thirteenth and walked, Cesar Geronimo pinch-ran, and he and Joe Morgan would both score in that half-inning.[30] Just as Dierker could smell his twentieth win, Fred Gladding and the bullpen gave up three runs in the bottom half, losing the game.[31] As much as the revenge no-hitter was an upward turning point, this game was just as much of a downward turning point for Houston. It proved to be the end of the pennant hopes for the Astros, but two more achievements were in store for Houston before the season's end. On September 19, the pitching staff broke the record for strikeouts in a season with their 1,123rd strikeout, a record that would stand for over twenty-five years. Larry Dierker, Don Wilson, and Tom Griffin all accumulated at least 200 apiece over the course of the season. The final exclamation point for the 1969 Astros came on September 30, when the Astros clinched their first non-losing season by winning their 81st game at Dodger Stadium.[32]

Meanwhile, the Mets, whom the Astros beat 10 out of 12 times that season, won the pennant. In fact, the Astros were the only team that had a winning record against them, with the Cardinals being an even .500 and everyone else having a losing record against New York. The Astros had shown some obvious improvement from the previous season's last place finish and 72 wins, but the team's sorrows were soured when their expansion mates, those Mets they had beaten so often that year, swept the Braves and took all but one game from the Baltimore Orioles to win an unexpected World Series title.

Houston fans now expected a contending ballclub when they went to the Astrodome in 1970, but despite the growth of 1969, there were still some internal holes that were festering. The front office had tried several players at first base without settling on one, even though Bob Watson was bouncing back and forth between the majors and minors, waiting for his shot. Guys like Chuck Harrison, Eddie Mathews, Rusty Staub, Doug Rader, Nate Colbert, Donn Clendenon, and Curt Blefary were considered for the position, and before 1970, Spec Richardson brought along another veteran first baseman in the form of Joe Pepitone. Like many guys, Pepitone did not get along well with Harry Walker, and having two stubborn minds coming from opposite directions only added to the upset churning of the clubhouse morale. When the Astros landed in Philadelphia before a series beginning on June 16, he was arrested over failure of alimony payments.[33] Only then was Bob Watson entrusted with the first base position full-time, and he came through. Joining him at first base was lefty-hitting John Mayberry, who would play in 50 games in 1970, the most he would play in a season in Houston.

The regular season began on April 7, but the season's highlights for the Astros began in an exhibition game on April 3. Against the Yankees, Doug Rader hit a home run into the Astrodome's upper deck off Stan Bahnsen, becoming the first player to ever do that. The team headed off to San Francisco to begin the regular season, and Larry Dierker took advantage of his second career Opening Day start as he beat the Giants. After dropping the next two, the home opener was next against the Braves. In the third inning of the third game, Jimmy Wynn launched his second home run of the game that not only brought in Norm Miller, but also soared a few rows above where Doug Rader's exhibition home run landed in the gold Upper level. Wynn's blast was the first to reach the upper deck in a regular season game. This feat was never again repeated by an Astro hitter. Not long after this game, Rader and Wynn were honored by the Astros when the cushioned seats their upper deck homers landed in were painted with appropriate illustrations, Rader's seat with a red rooster and Wynn's with a cannon. A short photoshoot with each seat was done with both players to further commemorate the outstanding achievements.

The eccentric Joe Pepitone was not a fit for Houston when he clashed with manager Harry Walker and had to briefly leave the team when arrested on the road.

Players with two of the most iconic nicknames in Astros history were the first two guys to knock home runs into the upper deck of the Astrodome, and they were memorialized with paintings appropriate for their aliases on the seats their respective long balls landed in.

On May 14, owner Judge Roy Hofheinz suffered a stroke.[34] This added another concern of Hofheinz's fitness to run the team as his financial status was entering into question by some. The opening of the Astrodome in 1965 sparked a lot of attendance, even over one million fans a year for a few years, which brought in a lot of revenue. Of course, it was during that same year that Bob Smith and Paul Richards departed, leaving only Hofheinz as the final juror to decide how to spend money. Rather than prioritizing a winning ballclub on the field, he invested in furthering the entertainment value of the area surrounding the Dome, known as the AstroDomain. Such amenities included the AstroHall, AstroWorld, the AstroWorld Hotel, and even the Ringling Bros and Barnum and Bailey Circus (Some critics remarked that he already owned a circus). These ventures were being built just as the Dome itself was beginning to no longer be enough to attract mass attendance and Houston fans were becoming hungry for a winner. As the spending of money increased while revenue at the ticket office decreased, financial struggles were inevitable, and that concern came up even before the stroke.[35]

The struggles against the Braves in 1969 shifted to the Reds in 1970 as Houston ended with the same 3-15 record they had against Atlanta the season prior. The third game of the May series between the two teams in Houston saw the Reds score fourteen runs, the most that would be scored against the S'tros this season, though that would be repeated two more times. The second time fourteen runs were scored off Astro pitching occurred after getting swept in two in a four-game series loss in New York to end the month of May. The Mets took the first game of a doubleheader on May 31 by the same 14-3 score the Reds put up a week earlier.[36]

A series in Atlanta in June only allowed for one Astros win, but it was notable. On Saturday, June 20, young Dominican outfield prospect Cesar Cedeno was called up to make his Major League debut. His hype was reflected by him batting third and in center field in the starting lineup. He collected two singles to get his first big league hit to begin a career that had the potential to rival the best players in the game's history. The series in Atlanta was also noteworthy as Bob Watson had taken over first base in the previous series in Philadelphia, and he got a hit in each game.

On June 21ˢᵗ, the day of the last game of the series in Atlanta, Jim Bouton, a relief pitcher who had been acquired the previous August, had his tell-all diary from the previous season, *Ball Four*, published. Players across baseball condemned the book as being intrusive, especially the Astros since the book's last month and a half covered their exploits. No such explicit account had been published before, and the clubhouse was now very weary of what they said and did around Bouton, which they felt was unfair to them. These feelings around Bouton persisted until he was demoted to Oklahoma City in late July due to poor performance and then released on August 12 as Bouton decided to retire from baseball. He became tired of his subpar pitching and his ostracization from the fallout of his book.

The streaky season continued until the end, with the season ending with the team's longest winning streak of 1970. Beginning with three in Atlanta and four back home against the Giants to end the season, the Astros pulled off seven in a row. During the first game of a doubleheader in San Diego on September 7, starting pitcher Ken Forsch made his first MLB appearance, going the distance to collect his first win.

The 1970 Houston Astros finished with a 79-83 record, regressing from 1969's even record of 81-81, but like 1967, there were some good individual performances. Doug Rader had his career year, having come through when the team needed him and having his batting average of .252 match his power numbers of 25 home runs. He also drove in 87 runs and won his first Gold Glove at third base. Cesar Cedeno finished his first big league season with a

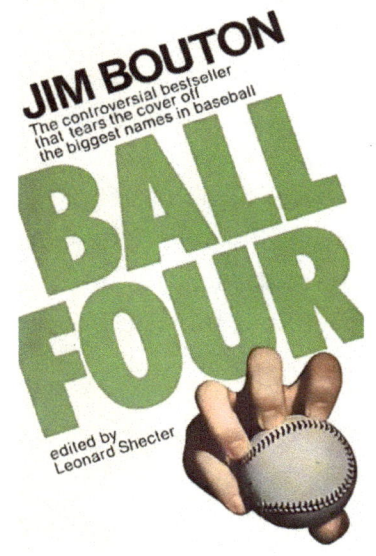

Relief pitcher Jim Bouton's infamous bestseller Ball Four caused strife in the Astros clubhouse and resentment towards him across baseball in 1970 for exposing the innermost details of the life of a professional athlete.

.310 batting average, 7 home runs, and 42 RBI in 90 games. The team's batting average was up nineteen points, and the offense set franchise-highs in grand slams (5) and stolen bases (114) in a season, but the team's ERA was also up 63 points. Larry Dierker won 16 games, but there was not much else to glamour at regarding the pitching staff.

Going into 1971, the Astros were still saddled with the duties of Harry Walker as the manager and Spec Richardson as the general manager. Still without Jerry Grote, Sonny Jackson, Dave Giusti, Bob Aspromonte, Mike Cuellar, and Rusty Staub, the fans of Houston were hoping that the remaining core of Jimmy Wynn, Joe Morgan, Bob Watson, Doug Rader, Larry Dierker, and Don Wilson could produce winning baseball, and they were becoming less patient for it. 1969 brought them a glimpse of success, and the team knew they should be achieving more, but no matter how controllable the reasons for them underperforming were, they were still present, as were by now rats underneath the lower grandstand of the luxurious Astrodome. While the Dome was beginning to show age, Dodger Stadium, which was three years older, was home to a winner and was still pristine.[37] In a season that you will find could have been one of the most successful and exciting in Astros history, those stumbling blocks continued to come between Houston and a championship ballclub.

THE 1971 SEASON

MARCH
SPRING TRAINING

Just as they had since 1964, the Astros' franchise hosted their Spring Training in the Grapefruit League in Florida, specifically out of Cocoa Beach at the Cocoa Expo Sports Center. The main ballpark at the complex was Cocoa Expo Stadium, where before the 1965 season, Bob Watson saw grounds crew members with pistols in the outfield seeking and killing snakes hiding in the grass. Everyone knew when another one had been found when an outfielder came sprinting into the infield screaming.[1]

Manager Harry Walker was optimistic about his team's chances of playing a large role in September because he remembered the fine season of 1969 despite a poor April and September, as well as a good 1970 despite down years from a few key players. Walker had also tried to cultivate a more positive atmosphere in Spring Training camp, including doing away with curfew for the regular season and the "Astro Mile," which players would have to run in six minutes or less. If the positivity could feed into the regular season and everyone could play at their best for the entire season, the belief was in pennant contention.[2]

However, before that could begin, second baseman Joe Morgan was holding out for more money before reporting to Cocoa.[3] This was a move that had previously gotten guys like Rusty Staub traded, as the front office did not want players who went against their wishes. Still, Morgan tried for "the big bundle"[4], and at one point he and general manager Spec Richardson were believed to be between $10,000 and $15,000 apart in negotiations.[5] On March 4, over a phone call with Richardson, Morgan agreed to between $62,000 and $65,000,[6] a raise from $50,000 in 1970, and he reported to Cocoa Beach.[7]

The next day, the Astros began their Spring Training schedule of exhibition games by welcoming the Boston Red Sox to Cocoa, where the left field fence had been moved in by 30 feet to help Cocoa hitters.[8] The BoSox took the Grapefruit League opener 4-3 against minor leaguer

Larry Yount, ace Larry Dierker, and bullpen arm George Culver.[9] All three pitchers were scheduled to pitch the game, rather than just the one starting pitcher. Walker, however, was pleased with how his team played as both outfielder Cesar Cedeno and shortstop Roger Metzger made great defensive plays. Metzger ended the game with a base hit during which he rounded first base too far and was thrown behind and tagged out. Walker believed that could be worked on, and many sportswriters were now believing that Metzger would not only win the starting shortstop job over Denis Menke, but that he would be the big piece that would put the

The Astros held their Spring Training in Cocoa, Florida, where somewhat cramped barracks for the players gave players distinctive memories of the complex.

Astros in contention for the pennant.[10]

The next stop was Fort Myers to take on the Kansas City Royals, where the Astros won in 11 innings.[11] The team's Spring schedule consisted of a win over the Atlanta Braves on March 9, a win over the Montreal Expos on the 13th, a loss to the Royals the next day, a win over the Cincinnati Reds the day after that, a loss to the Expos on the 18th, a win over the Minnesota Twins on the 20th, a win over the Los Angeles Dodgers on the

23rd, a loss to the Philadelphia Phillies on the 25th, a loss to the Dodgers on the 28th, and a loss to the Red Sox on the 29th.[12]

Despite Houston's Major League Baseball team being in Florida in March, there was still action inside the Astrodome on March 25 and 27. The NCAA Men's Basketball Final Four and championship games were hosted by Houston and played in the Dome, with the center court logo based very closely off of the Astros' primary logo, which showcased the Astrodome being orbited by baseballs inside of an orange circular background. Villanova defeated Western Kentucky and UCLA beat Kansas, so the championship featured Villanova vs UCLA. By just six points, UCLA scraped past Villanova for the ultimate prize.

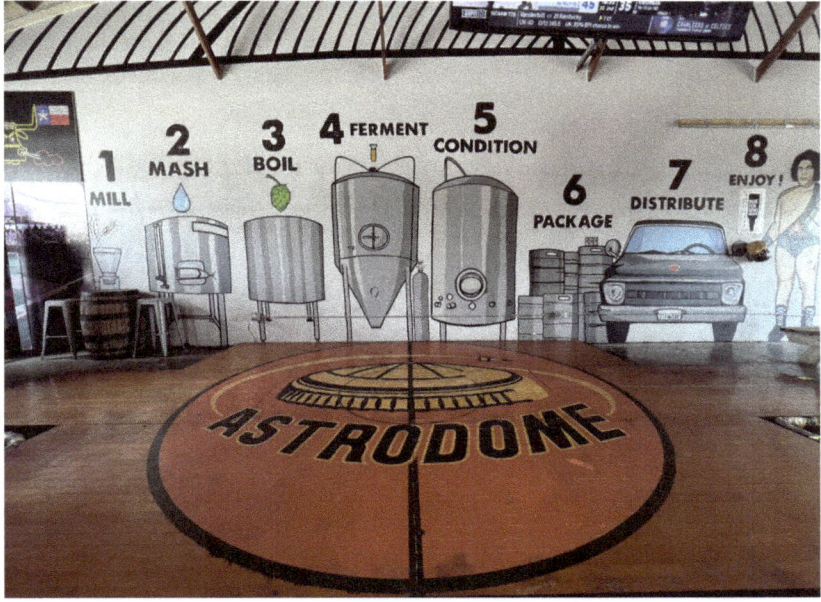

Midcourt during the 1971 NCAA Final Four creatively reflected the logo of the host's primary tenant.

Before reporting to Cocoa, Jimmy Wynn had a troubling offseason that saw his marriage hit its lowest low. He and Ruth had been having issues getting along in years prior, but one argument on the evening of December 21 turned out to be one more too many, as they went into the kitchen and Ruth grabbed a kitchen knife and punctured his stomach.

The stab wound turned out to be superficial, and Wynn was physically fine after surgery. He decided that it was time to move on from Ruth, so they got a divorce, and Wynn became concerned about being able to see his children.[13]

The thoughts surrounding this ordeal followed Wynn to Cocoa, but he hoped that playing baseball again would put him in a familiar setting and allow him to escape the turmoil in his own head. During the previous season, when Cesar Cedeno was called up, Wynn was moved to left field since Cedeno was believed to be the next big-time center fielder in baseball. Some news sources said that Wynn was unhappy with the position move, but in his autobiography, he says that he did not mind the switch, and that most of his mental energy was being spent on his failing marriage and dealing with Harry Walker every day.[14] His mood was not helped by Jim Bouton's diary *Ball Four* being published, which he and others felt intruded clubhouse privacy. However, Walker decided to put Wynn back in center field for the Spring to get his morale up, and they both spoke of that being the case. Walker believed that Wynn feeling better would trickle down to the rest of the team, and along with the addition of Metzger, would give the Astros a very good chance to win the division.[15]

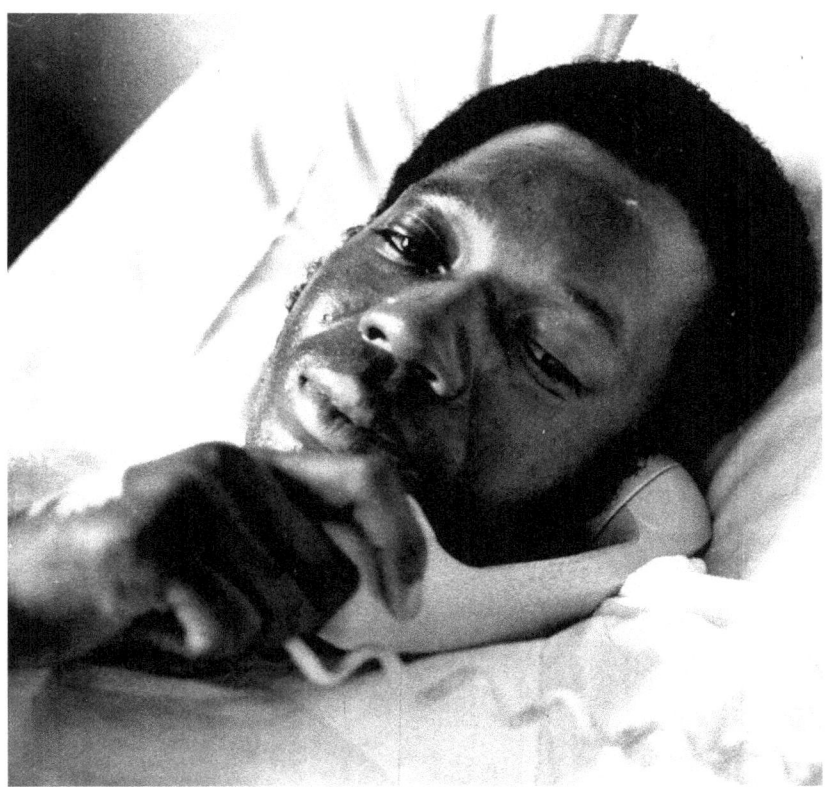

Outfielder Jimmy Wynn entered Spring Training desperate to find solace in playing baseball to escape the pain of his offseason stabbing and subsequent divorce.

Another outfielder that was popping up in conversation around the Astros' camp was the young Cesar Geronimo, whom the team acquired from the Yankees in an offseason draft before 1969 and had spent time with the big club in 1969 and 1970. His 2 RBI single in the ninth inning helped beat the Braves on March 9, and as his confidence rose, so did his likelihood of him having a definite role with the team for 1971.[16] Geronimo, nicknamed "Chief," was blocked by Cedeno in center field and Wynn in left field, while Jesus Alou was the frontrunner for right field, and Bob Watson and Norm Miller competed for the remaining out-field roster spot, but his speed and defensive ability would prove effective as a late-inning upgrade.

Two spots in the infield were locked down: Joe Morgan had second base well in his grasp by now, having stolen 42 bases in 1970. The "Red Rooster" Doug Rader had quickly emerged as the starting third baseman after fan-favorite Bob Aspromonte was traded in 1968. The other two positions of shortstop and first base had two or three candidates vying for the starting role in Spring Training. Roger Metzger began to emerge as the favorite for shortstop, with Denis Menke behind him because of his .306 batting average in 1970. Due to the likelihood of Metzger winning the shortstop job, Menke was trying out first base so his bat would remain in the lineup. Bob Watson was the highest-ranked natural first baseman trying for the position, and John Mayberry was behind him. Watson could also play left field, and Menke was even considered for the outfield as well.

Behind the plate, it was believed that the Astros had their strongest catching core in franchise history up to that point. Johnny Edwards was the frontline catcher, with newly acquired Jack Hiatt followed by the young Larry Howard. Edwards had long been considered one of the best defensive catchers in the National League, Hiatt had gotten experience with the Angels, Giants, Expos, and Cubs before being purchased by Houston, and Howard batted .307 in 31 games in 1970.[17] Having this high-level backstop trio would help the team's talented pitchers be even better.

That pitching staff was led by Larry Dierker, Don Wilson, Wade Blasingame, and Jack Billingham in the rotation, with Ken Forsch having debuted the September prior with success The Astros' 1970 season showcased more of the hitters than the pitchers, but this was still a strong staff consisting of a 20-game winner, a no-hit pitcher, and pennant race veteran, a talented finesse arm, and a potential overpowering young guy with a large build. The bullpen was anchored by closer Fred Gladding, and preceded by Buddy Harris, Denny Lemaster, George Culver, and Jim Ray. Tom Griffin was still on the staff, and there were some young farmhands such as Scipio Spinks, Ron Cook, Bill Greif, J.R. Richard, Skip Guinn, and Larry Yount, the older brother of future Hall of Famer Robin Yount.

The Astros clubhouse was another strength for the ballclub. With characters like Doug Rader, Norm Miller, George Culver, Fred Gladding, and others who tagged along with them, the team stayed loose and enjoyed every day they played. The players were grateful to be in the big leagues and they played hard-nosed. Joe Morgan was a level-headed homegrown player who helped mediate tension between Harry Walker and other players he had trouble with. Johnny Edwards and Denis Menke provided veteran leadership. Larry Dierker and Don Wilson took the ball every chance they could and were determined to prove themselves rightly as two of the best pitchers in the league. Dierker was even trying his hand at songwriting, penning tunes that the team sung together and rallied around for their amusement, especially when the lyrics were at Harry Walker's expense. Jack Billingham and Ken Forsch were young pitchers who worked hard. Culver, who spent time with six Major League clubs, said he had more fun with the Astros than he did with any other team.[18] The Astros were together on and off the field, even going out in large groups after games to bars and restaurants and such (That is, when curfew was not in effect).

The Astros organization had been seeking young talent through their scouting and development ever since the franchise was established as the Colt 45s and Paul Richards gained the reigns as general manager. From 1961 to 1973, the Colt 45s/Astros organization signed and developed more future Major League players than any other team, and the 1971 Astros showcased several of them.[19] Because of the poor dealings done by the front office led by Spec Richardson in years prior, there would be struggles during the 1971 season that perhaps the likes of Rusty Staub in right field, Mike Cuellar taking the ball every fourth or fifth day, Jerry Grote catching, Sonny Jackson at shortstop, or Dave Giusti closing out a game on the mound would have helped or even prevented. During the Spring, had Staub still been on the Astros, the outfield would not be in question at all, with Jimmy Wynn likely shifting over to left field so Cesar Cedeno could take over center, and Staub in right. The same goes for the shortstop position had Sonny Jackson been kept around to develop in Houston. Menke would not have been acquired, and likely neither would Metzger been gotten since there was no Joe Pepitone to trade for him. There would not have been a Pepitone because before that there would have been no Curt Blefary to trade for him, and the Astros would not have had Blefary because even before that, they would not have traded Mike Cuellar.

The rotation would have likely also been set sooner in the Spring with Cuellar still an Astro. Him, Dierker, Wilson, Griffin, and Forsch would round out a rotation, and as for Dave Giusti, he and Fred Gladding could have competed for the role of closing pitcher, with the other becoming the setup man.

Finally, with a different manager, the team would have had a better mentality, one more conducive to winning. Both Norm Miller and Scipio Spinks spoke of this complacency by the Astros during this time. Miller recalls that when a double play was in order, Walker would remind his fielders to get at least one out, which the team hated because they wanted to have the winning mindset of getting both outs.[20] Spinks said "The Astros taught me how to play; the Cardinals [The team he was traded to for the 1972 season] taught me how to win." He also spoke of how the Astros would go into a city with a good ballclub for a four-game series and have the goal of winning at least two of the games, while the Cardinals went in not only aiming but expecting to take all four.[21]

But alas, those assets were long gone by now, and Harry Walker had to put together what he had and field a quality Major League ballclub. And in a lot of respects, he did.

APRIL

FRESH ORANGE SLICES

anager Harry Walker believed that his ballclub for 1971 had its "best chance ever" to be successful, especially now that Joe Morgan's holdout was over, and he was signed and ready to play second base again. Jimmy Wynn was ready to put his offseason woes behind him and have another great season.

During the Astros Press Weekend, Doug Rader noticed that everyone on the team shared optimism for their chances to go deep into the postseason, saying "We all feel that we can go all the way, something that could have been absent in the past. Everyone this year seems to have a good attitude and an equally strong desire to play as a team." Johnny Edwards believed that as long as the pitching stayed strong and improved like he felt they could, that they would "be battling Cincinnati and Los Angeles for the National League Western division title." Gordon Verrell, a writer for the Independent in Long Beach, California, ironically predicted the Astros to win the division–for the second year in a row–and for the Dodgers to finish behind them in second place.[1] The theme of the Press Weekend was "Wait Til This Year," and everyone around the Houston ballclub believed that that's all they would have to do.[2]

Before Opening Day, the Astrodome hosted a few exhibition games, one on April 1 against the Yankees which the hometown team won 9-3, followed by a triple-header of five-inning games on the 2nd.[3] During these three games, general manager Spec Richardson experimented with a "points" system in determining winners of games, rather than runs.[4] The Astros took the first game against the Yankees 2-1, then the Twins took the field to face New York and won 4-1. Houston then came back to face the Twins as the Astros won the day by beating the Twins by a score of 5-3.[5] This gave the Astros a winning record for the exhibition season. Also on April 1, some news outlets reported that Larry Dierker had been traded to the Los Angeles Dodgers in exchange for Dick Allen, as an April Fool's joke.[6]

During the past two seasons, April had not been kind to the Astros, with the team going 4-20 during the first month of the season in 1969 and 7-14 in April of 1970. Walker said that he wanted his club to avoid those "April doldrums" as despite the Astros playing winning baseball after April in both 1969 and 1970, they could not make up the distance that slow starts had created.[7]

Houston fans got to experience Opening Day at home in the Astrodome for the first time in the 1970's decade, after the team began the season on the road the prior two seasons, coincidentally both times in California (San Francisco in 1970 and San Diego in 1969). This time, a different California team was starting their season in Houston as the Los Angeles Dodgers' manager Walter Alston tabbed Bill Singer as their Opening Day starting pitcher, while the Astros' Harry Walker went with his ace Larry Dierker to make his third career Opening Day start and his second in a row. Dierker only beat the Dodgers in LA once in his career, but he had better luck against his hometown team in Houston, which continued in this April 5 night game as his Astros started the season on the winning side of the ledger by a score of 5-2, a split that will come back into play a few games from now.[8]

Fans who were in attendance this day, and others who had read the newspaper and kept up with Astros news, easily noticed the different looking uniforms the Astros were now wearing compared to the prior seasons from 1965 to 1970. Navy caps in the team stores inside the Astrodome were now on sale at half price to clear the way for the new additions.[9] The "shooting star" jersey wordmark, as well as the primary logo as a patch on the left sleeve and the number font–varsity block–at home was the same, and the home jerseys were still made of genuine wool baseball flannel by Wilson Sporting Goods. What was now different was the inversed colors, with orange now being the primary color of the cap, undershirt sleeves, lettering and numbering, belt, and stirrup socks, while navy blue was now the secondary color, coloring the star on the cap and socks, streaks following the shooting star on the front of the jersey above the chain-stitched "ASTROS" script, outline of said script, and the trim around the numbers on the back. Joining the numbers on the back of the jersey for the first time in franchise history were last names, also orange and trimmed in navy blue, above the numbers. On the home jerseys, the names were cut and placed on the jersey in a radial arching fashion rather than conventional vertical arching, which simply takes the letter cut in a standard fashion and rounds them across the upper back of the jersey. Radial arching, contrary-wise, is a unique "typographic style in which each letter is custom-styled with its own degree of uphill or downhill slant," as they contour with an oval shape underneath the letters.[10] The jackets, however, were not updated until at least 1973, and they remained navy with the primary logo patch on the left chest, Texas state flag patch on the left sleeve, and orange stripes with white featheredges on the neck, sleeve, and bottom cuffs. When the jackets turned orange a year or two later, the shooting star replaced the circular logo on the chest, and the cuffs remained the same.

Considering Judge Hofheinz's tendency to make decisions that would make him more money, it is a little surprising that he would allow for last names on the backs of his players' jerseys as that feature somewhat negates the selling of scorecards as it negates the phrase "You can't tell the players without a scorecard" that vendors typically shout when advertising the team publications in the ballpark. As well, with Judge Hofheinz's innovation and creativity, it is also surprising that he did not make orange the primary color in the uniform sooner than 1971.

The 1971 Houston Astros showcased orange predominantly throughout their uniform, a first in Major League Baseball history.

The Astros had already made MLB uniform history in 1965 when the shooting star design debuted, as they became the first MLB team with a space-themed identity and the first to have an embroidered logo on the stirrups, and now they were the first big league team to wear orange as its primary accent color on the uniform. Regarding the stirrups, catcher Johnny Edwards recalls management requiring players to have the bottom of their pants at least high enough to show all the white of the sanitary sock underneath the stirrups.[11] Jerry Reuss, who arrived in Houston in 1972, railed on general manager Spec Richardson's policy of mandating not only the whole stirrup cut to be visible, but also the star, since he wanted the Astros' socks to look similar to those of the Cincinnati Reds, which like the Chicago Cubs as well, were notable for their low cuts that showed white sanitary sock less than halfway up the calf. In a time during which players were beginning to pull their stirrups up higher than the traditional 50/50 look of equal stirrup and sanitary sock showing, Richardson sent clubhouse attendant Whitey Diskin to the clubhouse one day to remove all the socks from the lockers and replace them with new pairs that had not been stretched, cut, or doctored in any other way. This worked until Cesar

Cedeno eventually set his mind to not wearing that look and continued sporting high cuts until Richardson decided to abandon his effort.[12]

Speaking of the Reds, just as they were toying around with the idea of red shoes in 1971, former Reds pitcher George Culver, now an Astro, took to the field in batting practice one day alongside Jimmy Wynn decked out in orange tennis shoes to try to get the team to think more about wearing orange shoes. Richardson saw them and called down to the field to tell them to get off the field with the non-black footwear.[13]

Whether a player was wearing his stirrups correctly or not, the new visual identity was ripe for a team that entered a season with optimism for perhaps the first time in years. Viewers with color televisions could now toggle through games and know that if they saw orange, especially if against the backdrop of bright green AstroTurf, it was the Houston Astros.

In the first inning, both Bob Watson and Denis Menke hit back-to-back RBI ground outs to get on the board early 2-0. Two innings later in the bottom of the third, Menke tripled in Joe Morgan and Watson to double the Houston scoring to 4, though the Dodgers had scored one an inning prior. The next inning, Cesar Cedeno brought in Johnny Edwards with a single into left field. Defense was also on display to further justify the high spirits going into the season, as both Jimmy Wynn and Cesar Geronimo threw out Dodger runners: Wynn throwing out Bill Russell at the plate in the third inning, and Geronimo throwing out Duke Sims at third base in the ninth. Dierker went the distance for a complete game, typical for him, and only surrendering one more blemish in the form of an RBI base hit by star Dodger shortstop Maury Wills. In the ninth inning, pinch-hitter Jim Lefebvre grounded back to Dierker, who threw to first base, manned by Menke this day as Watson was in left field, and despite being out-hit 10 to 5, Dierker and the Astros won 5-2, a split that would come into play again in a few days, and were tied with the Atlanta Braves for first place in the National League West division to begin the season.

It was Don Wilson's turn on the mound the next day against Claude Osteen, but while Wilson gave up half as many hits as Dierker did the day before, his one blemish on the day surrendered the same amount of runs that Dierker had, as Dodger right fielder Bill Buckner hit a two-run home run, his first of his career, that made up all the scoring in the game. The attendance was around half that of Opening Day, with only 11,883 Houstonians coming out to the Dome compared to 22,421 to start the season the day before. Nevertheless, in just under two hours, the Dodgers had their first win of 1971. After the game Buckner, beginning his rookie season after just a cup of coffee in the prior two seasons, said that if Wilson was one of the best pitchers in the league (Which he was considered at the time) that he was going to do very well. Wilson read that in the newspaper, and Joe Morgan could sense by the way his eyes were glaring at that paper that Buckner was in trouble.[14]

In the third game, after Jimmy Wynn hurt his back during his first inning at-bat in which he walked, Jesus Alou took his place and proceeded to hit three singles and bring in the deciding RBI in a quiet 2-1 game to win the opening series on April 7. Roger Metzger also collected a single for his first big league hit. An odd thing happened when Dodgers catcher Bill Sudakis lost a contact lens on the AstroTurf but none of the Dodgers or umpires could find it, so Sudakis had to leave the game in the fifth inning. The Astros welcomed Metzger's former team, the Chicago Cubs, into the Dome the next day to begin a four-game series, much to the Cubbies' chagrin. Despite the Cubs being in contention in 1969 and 1970 and having the likes of Hall of Famers Ernie Banks, Ron Santo, Billy Williams, and Fergie Jenkins, the better team did not always win in the Astrodome. While the Astros were built around pitching, defense and speed, the Cubs tended to wait for the big hit to score runs.[15] Wynn also had a great 1970 season against them. As a result, the Cubs only won 17 of the 52 games they had ever played in the Dome, including the first four games between the two clubs in 1971. That made for a .327 winning percentage indoors.[16]

In the last game of the first series of the season, Bill Sudakis of the Dodgers lost a contact lens on the Astro Turf but had to depart the contest when it could not be retrieved.

This trend continued during the second series of the season when the Astros took three of four against Chicago under the roof. Joe Pepitone, who joined the Cubs from Houston in the middle of 1970, was booed each time he came to the plate.[17] Cubs' starter Milt Pappas pitched well in the second game of the series, as well as helped himself with an RBI double, to earn a 6-0 win on April 9, as the Chicago lineup took advantage of Tom Griffin's rough day that saw Ken Forsch replace him in just the second inning. The next day, a rattled Fergie Jenkins single-handedly lost the game in the bottom of the ninth. With the bases loaded and one out, and the score 1-0 Cubs, Jenkins balked to allow Cesar Cedeno to score. Johnny Edwards was then intentionally walked to set up the double play, then Jenkins caught a pop fly back to him and threw to third base in an attempt to double up Cesar Geronimo, but the throw missed its target and Geronimo was able to come home and score the winning run.[18] The hometown team finished the opening homestand with Don Wilson's first win of the season, and the Astros would get on the plane to St. Louis with a 5-2 record and a tie for first place.

The fast start was covered foremost in the April edition of *Astro-Graphs*, the official publication of the Houston Sports Association (HSA). On the first page, it said that if the Astros continued the 5-2 ratio throughout all their home games (Or "Dome games," as they were sometimes referred to as), the team would have an overall home record of 58-23, six games better than the best home record the Astros had set back in 1969 of 52-29. The fans were already excited for the season to get underway because of the increased likelihood of them seeing a winning ballclub for the first time, and after that first homestand, they really got into it by creating signs and banners to hang in the ballpark that said things like "GO GET' EM ORANGE CRUSH" or "BEAT THE CUBS ORANGE CRUSH."[19] "Orange Crush" supplanted "Glasshouse Gang" (A play on words based off of the 1940's 'Gashouse Gang' St. Louis Cardinals and the glass roof the Astros now played under) to become the team's unofficial nickname in the early part of the season due to the new orange-dominant uniforms and the fast start to the season, and after Doug Rader began referring to the team with the new nickname in the clubhouse, newspapers around the country would soon use it as an alternative to using Astros.[20] The Baytown Sun in Baymont, Texas, often used phrases such as "Orangemen" for the team, "Orange fire" for a scoring threat, or any other phrase they could conjure up using the word "orange."

ASTRO-GRAPHS

OFFICIAL PUBLICATION
HOUSTON SPORTS ASSOCIATION

"The name Astrodome belongs exclusively to Houston Sports Association, Inc.

| ASTRODOME | HOUSTON, TEXAS | APRIL, 1971 |

"ORANGE CRUSH" GETS OFF TO JUICY START!

This is the "Orange Crush" banner that appeared during the first home stand in the Astrodome. The new nickname seemed to be catching on with fans in a hurry.

The sign dangling from in front of the red mezzanine seats in left field said it all:
GO GET 'EM ORANGE CRUSH
It proclaimed this in big bold letters, obviously handprinted and homemade.

It's the unofficial but definitely (and apparently unanimously) popular nickname of the Houston Astros.

The Big Orange, off to a juicier start than ever before in Houston major league baseball history, is even more orange this year. Orange is the dominant color in the Astros' uniforms in '71.

For their coming out party, the Astros dumped the Los Angeles Dodgers, regarded by many baseball people as THE team to beat in the National League West this season.

The Astros took the opener and two out of three games from the Dodgers, then proceeded to wipe out Leo Durocher and the cantankerous Chicago Cubs in three out of four games to give them a 5-2 opening homestand.

The best total home season the Astros ever had was in 1969 when their record was 52-29 in the Astrodome. If the Astros could continue the 5-2 ratio throughout the home season it would give them about a 58-23 record in the Dome.

And, if the home record continues "rosy," part of the record may be attributed to fans' support with the banners about the Orange Crush.

Pitcher Larry Dierker (left) and catcher John Edwards show off the new Astro uniforms at a recent Astro Buddies meeting. The "civilian" is Astro broadcaster Loel Passe.

Some Home Games Show 'Different' Starting Times

Because of travel arrangements and other reasons, several Astros' home games have unusual starting times this season. They include: Sunday, May 2 (Mets, 3 p.m.); Monday, June 14 (Pirates, 7:05 p.m.); Monday, June 28 (Braves, twi-nighter, 6:30 p.m.); Saturday, July 17 (Mets, 5 p.m.); Sunday, July 18 (Phils, doubleheader, 1:30 p.m.); Tuesday, Aug. 3 (Cubs, 5 p.m.), and Saturday, Sept. 18 (Reds, 1:15 p.m.).

Otherwise, the standard Astrodome time structure will be in effect—Sunday home games starting at 2 p.m., all other games starting at 7:30 p.m.

Fans are reminded that free pocket schedules, listing all the "different" starting times are available throughout the Southwest, or by writing the Publicity Office at the Dome (Box 288, Houston, 77001).

500TH N.L. GAME IN DOME IN '71

The 1971 season marks an "anniversary" in Houston baseball—the 500th National League game to be played in the Astrodome.

Date of the 500th game—Friday, April 30, against the New York Mets.

The first official National League game in the Astrodome was played on April 12, 1965, with Philadelphia scoring a 2-0 victory over the Astros.

Chris Short was the winning pitcher, Bob Bruce the loser in that first game and Richie Allen homered for the two Phillie runs.

Two Twinbills Scheduled For Astrodome in '71

The Astros' 1971 home schedule includes a pair of special attractions for "dyed in the wool" baseball fans as well as for bargain-hunters.

Two regulation doubleheaders are scheduled in the Astrodome this year.

The first is a twi-night doubleheader against the Atlanta Braves, starting at 5:30 p.m. on Monday, June 28.

The second is an afternoon doubleheader against the Philadelphia Phillies, starting at 1:30 p.m. on Sunday, July 18.

Both games in each case will be regulation nine-inning contests.

The most recent Dome doubleheader was played last Aug. 3 against the Braves. Houston won the opener 7-5, Atlanta the second game 3-1.

At Busch Stadium, the team's visual identity on the road also supported the new Orange Crush moniker, with the same orange caps, undershirt sleeves, socks, and lettering on the Rawlings grey road uniforms also debuting away from Houston, though the number font abroad was the McAuliffe font, often known as the Red Sox font, rather than the varsity block font used at home. The Astros dropped the first game of the two-game series against the Cardinals 5-4 despite rallying to get two baserunners in the last inning and pitcher Wade Blasingame hitting the first Astros home run of the season. The Cardinals almost had a sweep on April 13 despite a 37-minute rain delay and the smallest crowd in the new Busch Stadium's history up to that point (5,605).[21] However, in the top of the ninth, down 4-3, the Astros set up Joe Morgan to knock a two-RBI single and Norm Miller to launch a three-run home run to deep right field, both with two outs, to win 8-4. The homer was Miller's first of the season, though it was the first of only two he would muster in 1971.[22]

Veteran pitcher Wade Blasingame led Houston pitchers in batting RBI in 1971, beginning with the first home run of the season for the Astros during the first road trip of the season.

The momentum kept the Orange Crush, well, crushing, even with Jimmy Wynn still hurt, as they went to San Francisco to take on the first-place Giants, who like the Dodgers, were also seen as a strong NL West contender.

Outfielder Norm Miller, normally a reliable athlete for Houston, saw less time on the field in 1971 and subsequently only hit two home runs but maintained his entertaining aura, a trait he shared with several other Astros.

Unfortunately, the momentum did not follow the Astros into California on April 14, as despite a Bob Watson home run in the first of the two games at Candlestick Park, Tito Fuentes walked off George Culver with a single in the eleventh inning, and Fran Healy walked off Jim Ray with a solo homer in the tenth inning of the next day's game to complete the two-game sweep. The Dodgers greeted the Astros with the same treatment, with Bill Buckner singling home Dick Allen in the bottom of the tenth to hand Culver another extra inning loss. The three straight losses had put the Astros at .500 with a 6-6 record, but that was not to be the case for long as pitcher Wade Blasingame singled in a run to help his winning cause the next day, and Jimmy Wynn crushed his first home run of the season into left field at Dodger Stadium. After a Doug Rader RBI triple and Joe Morgan sacrifice fly in the late innings, the Orange Crush was back in business with a 5-3 win. This continued in the fifth inning of the rubber match on the afternoon of Sunday, April 18. Five runs scored courtesy of a Joe Morgan home run (Three runs) and doubles from the Bull and the Red Rooster (One run apiece). In the sixth, Roger Metzger gave the Astros a team cycle with an RBI triple to score Jack Hiatt. Los Angeles scored two in the bottom of the ninth to try to come back, but Culver collected his second save to win the team's second series against the Dodgers.

It was during this series that Don Wilson attempted to get revenge on Bill Buckner for his snide comment in the paper after the second game of the season. Wilson first called the home clubhouse to invite Buckner to talk to him, but that was demonstrably declined when Buckner stayed in the clubhouse during batting practice and pregame warmups. Around the fifth inning, as Wilson walked towards the bullpen to throw between starts, as was typical back then, Buckner was warming up between innings in his position of right field, perfect placement for Wilson to dart directly toward him and chase the Dodger rookie around the outfield. Wilson did not get ahold of Buckner, but he made his point.[23]

Just as the Astros did at the beginning of the season, they followed their games with the Dodgers with games against the Cubs, with the Orange Crush making their first trip to Wrigley Field with their new look and optimism on April 20. Rich Chiles, a young outfielder who had been called up for this series, made his MLB debut in the top of the eighth inning when he lined into a double play while pinch-hitting for starting pitcher Tom Griffin.[24] Fergie Jenkins humbled the S'tros in the game, allowing one run and overcoming a balk in the ninth to win his second game of the season. Jenkins had now committed two balks in the first month of the 1971 season, both against Houston. Both were similar, but he vehemently disagreed with this one as he felt that he simply took a "second stare" in toward his catcher for the sign.[25]

After a rainout on April 21, Larry Dierker was the king of the hill on April 22 as he copied Jenkins' feat of only allowing one run, but Dierker did not commit a balk. He also singled and scored to help himself. Just as Ron Santo was the big bat for the Cubs on Tuesday, Bob Watson was the big stick for the winning Astros on Thursday as he supplemented Dierker's gem with his third homer of the season against 44-degree temperatures and stiff wind to score two runs.[26] The Astros had finished the road trip that took them from the Midwest to the West Coast and then back to the Midwest, and now they headed back to the South/Southwest

Rich Chiles debuted in the Major Leagues in Chicago with his first at-bat and collected his first hit and defensive innings in the Dome the following week.

for the weekend, where they would meet a team from not only a different region, but a different country.

From Montreal, Ontario, Canada came the Expos into the Astrodome, who were a half game out of first place in the NL East division. The Expos had just begun franchise play two seasons prior in 1969, so they were not seen as a threat to contending teams. However, they did have Rusty Staub in right field, whom they had acquired from Houston before the Expos' inaugural season. That trade is often cited as one of the worst trades Spec Richardson made as general manager, but Montreal loved having "Le Grande Orange" north of the border, since Staub assimilated with the culture seamlessly. He even learned French so he could speak to the fans at Jarry Park. Despite being on a lesser ballclub, Staub enjoyed playing for the Expos more than he did the Astros, as Montreal by comparison did not have a closed-minded general manager and a strict manager.

The Expos shocked baseball by sweeping the Astros in the Dome, including by beating Don Wilson in game one. Mike Marshall, whom the Astros had briefly for four games in 1970, saved the first two games for Montreal, both lost by a score of 3-2. Staub clubbed a two-run homer in the sixth to begin the scoring. The Houston highlight of game one was Chiles' first big league hit, a triple, and his first big league run scored after a Roger Metzger sacrifice fly to left field. In the second game Chiles almost had another triple, but after he was declared out at second base on appeal for not touching the base, the hit was only scored as a single. He got to grace the AstroTurf outfield for the first time in the eighth inning of the third game when he was brought in as a substitute in right field.

As much as the Astros had been hyping themselves up, this series loss seemed to set that back a little bit, as they had gone from second place with a winning record to fourth place and under .500. Montreal skipper Gene Mauch acknowledged that "a sweep in the Astrodome is a great feeling."[27]

Mauch's prior team, the Phillies, did not provide any immediate relief when they came into town, as they handed Houston its second straight 2-1 loss as the new week started on April 26. However, ace Larry Dierker's turn to take the ball came the next day, and as was typical for him, he went the distance and beat the Phils, filling the role of "stopper" for the team.[28] He only needed one run, which Doug Rader gave him in the bottom of the eighth when he brought in Denis Menke, who had just stolen third base off Phillies catcher Tim McCarver, on a sacrifice fly to center. That was Jim Bunning's only flaw of the night, as he also pitched a complete game.

The next night was also a hard-earned win, but the hitting had to come through to make it happen this time. Both sides traded blows until the bottom of the tenth, when Jimmy Wynn walked and Cesar Geronimo, who had entered the game as a pinch-hitter for Bob Watson back in the eighth, pulled a ball into right field that rolled long enough for him to make it to third base and Wynn to make it all the way home. Geronimo had put the Astros back at .500 with a walk-off triple.

Cesar Geronimo, still a young outfield prospect, drew attention in Spring Training for his speed and defense, and he helped the Astros beat the Phillies on a walk-off hit in late April.

A weekend series against the New York Mets began two days later on April 30, the 500th game in the Astrodome. That game also went extra innings, with the Mets pulling it out in twelve. Joe Morgan's eighth-inning home run tied the game at three, but only when Ken Boswell singled in Bud Harrelson in the twelfth did more action come around.

At the end of the first month of the 1971 season, the Houston Astros had a record of 11-12 and were in third place, seven games behind the first-place Giants and two-and-a-half behind the Dodgers. Despite the losing record and the feeling that perhaps the team should have been closer to first, if not in first, the first month was exciting, seeing as the Astros became the "Orange Crush" at the plate and proved to be playing as well as the clubhouse believed they could. Larry Dierker was 3-0 and had pitched at least eight innings in each of his five starts. Bob Watson was hitting .314 with three home runs and twelve RBI. The rest of the lineup did not have great numbers, but they felt that one-run losses were hurting them the most, and they were determined to start turning the tide in those close contests. They ended the month with seven straight one-run games, only winning two of them, but relief pitcher Jim Ray commented after Geronimo's walk-off game that "We've turned around. We are going to be winning from here on."[29]

Jim Ray was a reliable relief arm for the Astros in the past, but would solidify himself even more in 1971 by putting up a 10-4 record and 2.12 ERA.

MAY
CAUTIOUSLY OPTIMISTIC

Going into the second month of the season, the Astros were not exactly on fire, but the same preseason feelings that they could win were still felt by the clubhouse and fans, and other teams and writers around the league were beginning to take notice. Except for the sweep at the hands of the Expos, the team from the Space City was making it seem more likely than initially thought that they would be involved when it came to determining the NL West winner.

Just as he did to begin April, Larry Dierker turned in a complete game victory, allowing only two hits in the first eight innings and only one run in the ninth inning. Jimmy Wynn and Bob Watson each helped the cause with RBI singles in the first inning, and Joe Morgan took Mets ace Tom Seaver deep in the third to give Dierker all the runs he needed to seal a 3-1 win to put the team back at .500 at 12-12. Houston took the matchup of ace pitchers, but the Mets came out on top when the sidekicks took the mound on May 2, as neither Don Wilson nor Jerry Koosman could get a decision in regulation, and former Astro Ron Taylor took the win out of the bullpen. In the sixth inning, Cleon Jones, a former football halfback, scored on an Ed Kranepool single by colliding with catcher Jack Hiatt. Hiatt was attended to by the Astros' trainer before shaking off the blow and remaining in the game. Another former Astro, Bob Aspromonte, came through after Ken Boswell's double with another extra-base hit, a triple, to score Boswell as the winning run in the top of the tenth inning. The 4-3 loss ended a 3-6 homestand and sent the Astros to Montreal.

Two days off followed, the second of which Mother Nature decided they would have. Once the rain subsided, Wade Blasingame took the ball on Cinco de Mayo against Expos ace Bill Stoneman, who went the distance and only allowed a run when Jimmy Wynn scored on a wild pitch in the ninth inning. The Expos got their five runs in the first three innings, including a leadoff home run by Ron Hunt in the bottom of the first, and did not look back. With the extra days off, Dierker was able to pitch again on May 6, and he continued to be the go-to guy for the Astros as he turned the tide with a 5-2 win, his fifth in a row. A three-run first inning by his batting order helped him to pitch with confidence, and Denny Lemaster and Fred Gladding came on in the eighth and ninth to collect the hold and the save as the Orange Crush put together a good team win going into Philadelphia.

Houston's first series playing in the new Veterans Stadium in Philadelphia began on May 7 with Don Wilson and Jim Bunning starting for their respective clubs. In a rare baseball play, Wilson bunted a ball in the second inning that got between Bunning and third baseman Don Money, but neither of them could get to the ball until Johnny Edwards scored from second base and Wilson reached second himself. Money was charging in towards the plate and Larry Bowa was heading to third base to try for a play to throw Edwards out there, but instead, the ball was fielded by left fielder Larry Hisle, who had come all the way into the infield to corral the bunt. Joe Morgan went 4-for-4 with a double, 2 RBI, three runs scored, and two stolen bases as he and Wilson led the way to an 8-1 win in what he said was his first start since 1969 that he felt no arm discomfort.[1]

Rain postponed Saturday's game, but back home under the Dome, Johns Hopkins University defeated Navy in a lacrosse matchup.[2] When the Astros played again on Sunday, May 9, Tim McCarver batted in both runs the Phils scored, including the winning run in the bottom of the tenth off Denny Lemaster to diminish Johnny Edwards' RBI base hit in the eighth to plate Cesar Cedeno. The next day saw the Astros lose another one-run game by a 2-1 score in New York, followed by an 8-1 defeat on May 11 in which the Mets supported Nolan Ryan and gave Larry Dierker his first loss of the season after winning his first five starts.

Any pitcher is entitled to a rough start every now and then, and this was not Dierker's day as he only pitched five and two-thirds innings while allowing six earned runs on nine hits. Dave Marshall hit a grand slam off George Culver, who had just relieved Dierker, but the three runs that scored ahead of Marshall were charged to the Houston ace. Postgame, Dierker was accused of throwing at Marshall earlier in the game, adding frustration to his day. Dierker denied the claim, citing his stiffened elbow on this day.[3] This start might have been one that, the day afterward, he took some time to run a lot.

According to Dierker, when asked about his regimens for staying in shape and building strength, he did not have one per say, but he did have a practice he began about halfway into

The "Red Rooster" Doug Rader was primarily known for his Gold Glove-caliber defense at the hot corner, but he was also a very strong slugger in the batter's box, as well as one of the only Astros who benefited from manager Harry Walker's style.

his career. If he pitched poorly, he would punish himself the next day by running. And running. And running. This conditioned his mind to want to pitch well so he could take it easy the next day."[4] Since his career began in 1964 and ended in 1977, his career's halfway point was between 1970 and 1971, so he may have been doing his running after subpar starts by now, though if so, he did not have to do much of it at all in the first half of the 1971 season.

Houston salvaged the third game with the help of Doug Rader's three-run homer off Tom Seaver. Harry Walker mentored the third baseman about hitting for an hour in the skipper's hotel room the previous night to try to get out of an 0-28 slump. Despite his contempt for black players and those who did not follow his hitting style, those who were willing to listen to Walker often reaped benefits, as the next series would show again.

The Cardinals met the Astros in the Dome on May 14 for a weekend series, and Bob Gibson pitched the Cards to victory over Jack Billingham, as did Steve Carlton over Tom Griffin on May 15. However, on Sunday afternoon, it was Dierker's day once again. He did not pitch a complete game this time either, and he allowed thirteen hits, but only three runs and Jim Ray held it down over the last three innings. It turned out that the Astros' pitching did not need to do much to win on this day as Rader belted a grand slam deep into left field in just the first inning to begin an onslaught of the Orange Crush. Rader brought in two more runs with a double in the third inning to tie the franchise record of six RBI in one game. The Red Rooster's two-bagger was followed by Jesus Alou's RBI single to bring him around. Cesar Cedeno, Jimmy Wynn, and Denis Menke had their own RBI hits in the fourth, as did Roger Metzger in the fifth to score Dierker after he reached scoring position with a double. Metzger and Jack Hiatt each collected three hits as their team put up seventeen total hits, scoring twelve runs in doing so, to make the final score 12-4.[5] Rader credited his two-for-four day with six RBI to manager Walker's tips, and Wynn hoped that this would be a reignition of the team's hitting for the month of May.[6]

Don Wilson, who had won his last two starts, got the ball to greet the San Diego Padres in the first of four midweek contests. He pitched a complete game shutout and only allowed four hits to cruise to victory on May 18. Ken Forsch did not have quite the same luxury the next night in his first start of the season, but he did pitch eight innings of two-run ball, and his team still won when Denis Menke singled home Cesar Cedeno in the bottom of the ninth to walk it off. The Padres were the ones to pull it off late in the game on May 20, however, when Ollie Brown singled in

Nate Colbert in the tenth inning. Jack Billingham's seven-inning performance of four-hit, one-run pitching was spoiled by Fred Gladding, who surrendered the same amount of runs on half as many hits. On the other hand, Wade Blasingame only hurt himself when he started the fourth and final game of the series when he gave up three runs on five hits in six innings. Jesus Alou scored Roger Metzger in the second inning with a triple, but only after Nate Colbert's RBI three-bagger in the first. When Jimmy Wynn pinch-hit for Johnny Edwards and grounded out with runners on first and third in the bottom of the ninth, the Padres had won the game, and the series was split.

If the Astros were waiting for a big series to light them up, they would get one the weekend of May 21-23. The division-leading San Francisco Giants were coming to Houston, and they were ten-and-a-half games up on the fourth place S'tros and fresh off three straight series wins against the Reds and Dodgers at home, and most recently the Cubs to begin the road trip that now took them inside the Astrodome. These two teams had faced each other for a short two-game stint in April, with the Giants taking both, but on close walk-off wins. To prepare for these pivotal games, manager Harry Walker did two things: He called for a practice session late in the morning before the first game on Friday against the division leaders. Walker wanted to see if that could shake up the routine enough to put his players' minds in a different state. He also called up first baseman John Mayberry for the first time this season. At triple-A Oklahoma City, he was batting .376 with 18 RBI. Catcher Larry Howard was sent to OKC in return.[7]

The stopper Larry Dierker pitched the first game of the series for the Astros against Hall of Famer Gaylord Perry, and while he did not offer up his usual complete game, he came close, only giving up the ball to Fred Gladding with one out recorded in the ninth inning and winning 4-1. Roger Metzger, Norm Miller, and Johnny Edwards each batted in runs in the third and fourth innings, Miller's hit being a two-RBI double, and Gladding had as easy an outing a closer can have, getting a ground ball double play out of Al Gallagher, the only batter he faced, to close out the first game and give Dierker his seventh win. The Astros' ace was wearing the same pair of baseball spikes in every game he pitched so far this season and vowed to continue until his winning ways ceased. After this win against the Giants, during which he struck out Willie Mays twice, there was over an inch of the sole worn off on the inside of the shoes, but Dierker still did not discard them.[8]

Mayberry was lauded early on as a slugging first baseman that every team looks for, and he added reliable defense as well.

Catcher Larry Howard also provided depth at a strong position for the Astros in 1971.

Don Wilson started the Saturday game on May 22, and it was while he was up to bat in the third inning that Johnny Edwards stole home off Giants' pitcher Rich Robertson. Edwards had reached base via double and advanced to third on a passed ball by Dick Dietz. Seeing a catcher stealing home was surely a jarring sight for the Giants, but the Astros scored their first run of the ballgame thanks to the veteran's daring decision. Willie Mays, the man many writers were comparing the potential of Cesar Cedeno to, tied the game at one in the ninth by singling in Bobby Bonds, spoiling Houston's series win...for the time being. Fred

Gladding and George Culver kept the Giants at bay long enough to send the game into the twelfth inning, and after Joe Morgan and Jimmy Wynn both were retired by Don McMahon, Cedeno strolled up to the plate, He tried to check his swing but knocked the ball just over first baseman Willie McCovey's head and into right field for a double, setting up John Mayberry, who started at first base, to come up and knock a single into right-center field to score Cedeno and win the game in Mayberry's second big league game of the season.[9]

The Astros had won the series over the Giants, though the visitors did win the third game when Tom Griffin struggled through two innings for his fifth loss. An off day gave the Astros ample time to rest before beginning a road trip that would take them to four different cities and into the month of June. They would stop first in San Diego for three more games with the Padres, of which Houston would win all three, first on Tuesday, May 25, thanks to Edwards' three-run long ball in the seventh to put the Astros ahead. A doubleheader was on tap for May 26, with no umpire at second base for either game as Tony Venzon, the home plate umpire on Opening Day in the Astrodome, was forced away from baseball on this day due to health issues. He died on September 20 following open-heart surgery. Also strange was that Padre starter Al Santorini only pitched a third of an inning in the first game of the doubleheader, as Dave Roberts was brought in after that. Houston's pitcher Wade Blasingame, meanwhile, marked up one of the two RBI singles the Astros used to get their runs, with the other coming from Bob Watson. Doug Rader also went 3-for-4, scoring those two runs.

However, it did not come without a little drama for Harry Walker, as he expressed concern about the legality of Ivan Murell's Japanese-manufactured bat. At the time, American made bats had ends that were full, while Japanese bats had a half-sphere of wood shaved out of it to make a "cup" that is often seen on bats anywhere today. This was 1971 though, so Walker had his team play the rest of the game under protest, though it did not matter as his team took care of business anyways.[10]

Houston skipper Harry Walker was one of the two people involved with the Astros in the late 1960's and early 1970's that were most responsible for the underperformance of the team on the field, due to his closed-minded and racist attitude in the clubhouse and dugout.

It was much easier for the Orange Crush to do their thing in the second game. This time Santorini pitched six innings but allowed four runs (Two earned) on six hits. Only four of the Astros' eight runs scored with the use of hits. Rich Chiles plated Joe Morgan with a single in the fifth inning, and Johnny Edwards hit a bases-loaded, bases-clearing triple in the eighth. Guess who won that game on the mound? Once again, ace starting pitcher Dierker, presumably in the same worn-out spikes. He delivered a gem, throwing a one-hit shutout, the only hit coming with two outs in the seventh inning when Ollie Brown broke his bat on a weak hit up the middle into center field.[11] This was not the first time Dierker had come close to a no-hitter, as he lost one against the Mets in 1965 and one on September 13, 1969, in Atlanta. In the latter game, he pitched eight and two-thirds innings before Denis Menke's lazy throw did not reach first base in time to retire Braves' second baseman Felix Millan. Even after that, he still pitched three more innings and came three outs from his twentieth win of the season before the bullpen gave up the lead in an otherwise scoreless game through twelve innings.

This win in game two of the San Diego twin-bill was his first career one-hitter, and it put his team over .500 at 23-22.[12] Games like this are part of the reason why Dierker's favorite ballpark to pitch in on the road was San Diego's.[13]

May 27 was an off day from National League competition for the Houston Astros, but they were taking a quick stop on their way to Cincinnati. The team was to visit their triple-A affiliate, the Oklahoma City 89ers, for an exhibition game. Ken Forsch was expected to start on the mound.[14]

Former Astros skipper Grady Hatton was now a scout for the organization, and he knew that the Cincinnati Reds were not hitting very well when his team was due to visit beginning May 28 for four weekend games. Hatton was surprised about the lack of home run output from his club, as Joe Morgan led the team in long balls—with only three. The Toy Cannon, meanwhile, had only one up to this point.[15] However, Jesus Alou was batting .374, second in the NL and 134 points higher than the team's collective batting average.

Fans of pitcher's duels got exactly that in the first game, with Reds first baseman Lee May hitting a walk-off single to bring home Pete Rose…

in the thirteenth inning…to win the game for the Reds by a score of…1-0. Alou only mustered one hit and threw his helmet in frustration after his last time at bat in the thirteenth inning, possibly for receiving the take sign when the count was in his favor at 3 balls and one strike.[16]

Jimmy Wynn returned to his old ways on May 29 by batting in both Astros runs in a 2-1 win to back up starting pitcher Ken Forsch. Wynn hit a solo home run in the fourth inning and batted in Roger Metzger with a single in the sixth. It was by the same score that Cincinnati took game three of the series. John Mayberry hit his first home run of the season but could not corral a line drive towards him off the bat of left fielder Bernie Carbo that scored catcher Johnny Bench late in the game.[17] Another negative tidbit of Astros news was that George Kirksey, one of the founding members of the Houston Sports Association, which was instrumental in getting Houston an MLB team, had died after an accident in France.[18]

The "Toy Cannon" Jimmy Wynn, notorious for being an all-around player and unexpected home run hitter at his 5'9", 165lb frame, only trotted around the bases seven times in 1971.

To end the month, Larry Dierker, coming off a one-hitter in San Diego, took his start on May 31, a Monday, typically an irregular day to end a series, and brought his team back over .500 again with a 4-1 win on Memorial Day. Cesar Cedeno replaced Jimmy Wynn in the lineup at the last minute when Wynn determined that a sprained left wrist was too much to bear that day. Cedeno, who was just hitting .180 before Monday's game began, took full advantage, and showed once again the kind of player he would become by collecting three RBI on three hits, one of them a two-run homer. Joe Morgan added two hits, a stolen base, and a run scored when he came around before Cedeno on the latter's long ball. Four Astros also collected doubles: Doug Rader, Johnny Edwards, Bob Watson, and Cedeno's which brought in a run. Dierker helped himself by bringing home his catcher Johnny Edwards for the other run in the fourth inning.

Record-wise, May had been better for Houston than April, which given the success the team had in April, kept the optimism up in the clubhouse. A 14-12 record in the month put them at 25-24. Pitching coach Jim Owens began predicting that Dierker, whose ERA was at 1.86, would win 25 ballgames in 1971.[19] Ken Forsch was doing well in his starts as his ERA was even lower at 1.35. Don Wilson's was at a more modest 2.81 but had still won four games so far. Joe Morgan was now batting .261 to get closer to Bob Watson, who was at .277. However, neither of them could compare to Jack Hiatt's .400 average. Hiatt was not playing every day, but he was getting plenty of opportunities to give the veteran Johnny Edwards rest, and just as predicted before the season began, the Astros were not sacrificing production on those rest days thanks to Hiatt. Denis Menke was batting .252 when he was playing first base over Watson, and Cedeno looked like he would be coming out of his low .196 clip soon. The club was still in third place, but now eleven games out of first place. However, there were only two months down, and still four months to play, and the highs of solid pitching and periodic onslaughts of hitting kept the clubhouse feeling like they were still in it to win.

Pitching coach Jim Owens predicted that starting pitcher Larry Dierker would win 25 games in 1971 after the ace had the most wins and lowest ERA in the National League through the first two months of the season. Notice Dierker wearing his pants and stirrup socks the way general manager Spec Richardson required, as well as the worn-out shoes he kept wearing while he was winning early in the season.

JUNE

ROUGH STREAKS

A long road trip continued into the season's third month when the Astros took a third stop at a division rival's ballpark, this time in Atlanta to see the Braves for the first time. Throughout all of Houston's Major League history, the Braves have been a thorn in the Astros' side, and that continued to begin June of 1971, but not at first. Cesar Cedeno, who made his big league debut in Atlanta the previous June in 1970 in center field and batting third, hit well in Atlanta, and it showed on June 1 when he collected four hits in five trips, including a two-run home run and RBI double. He both batted in and scored three runs, meaning all but one of the Astros' seven runs were to Cedeno's credit. He said after the game that all his hits came with two strikes, and the homer was off a hanging curveball.[1]

The next two games went the Braves' way, 3-1 and 5-2. Cedeno made three great catches in center field in the second game, including one to rob Hal King of a home run. King, using a Dave Marshall-model bat, lifted another fly ball in that game that hit the right field club level façade for a homer. Over the course of the series, Braves center fielder Sonny Jackson only managed one hit. This is the same Sonny Jackson who the Astros had signed in 1963 and finished second in 1966 Rookie of the Year voting by batting .292 with 49 stolen bases. Demonstrably, his performance dropped off after moving to Atlanta, proving that the hitter's ballpark nicknamed the "Launching Pad" was not well-suited to Jackson's playing style the way the spacious and quick-surfaced Astrodome was.

After the series loss in the South, the Astros went from the frying pan into the fire when the schedule listed Pittsburgh as the fourth and final stop of the trip. The Pirates, a team Jimmy Wynn performed well against the year prior, welcomed Houston into Three Rivers Stadium on June 4 for the weekend, and for the second day in a row, two runs were not enough to get a win as the Pirates scored three, which was also how many games the Astros had now lost in a row. The next day proved that twice as many runs were enough. Larry Dierker worked around a triple by Pirates pitcher Steve Blass and a sacrifice fly by Dave Cash to bring him home, to keep the Bucs at bay and allow for RBI singles from Jack Hiatt, Bob Watson, and Cesar Cedeno to make the difference, with another run scoring on a wild pitch. Pirates' catcher Manny Sanguillen picked Hiatt off second after his RBI hit, as part of a "strike 'em out, throw 'em out" double play, but the Astros still won 4-1, and Dierker reached double digits in victories on the season. He had now begun the 1971 season with a 10-1 record and was a huge part of keeping the Astros winning as often as they were.

However, as it had seemed so far, when Dierker was not on the mound, it could be a struggle to make good things happen. The Pirates won the series by beating Wade Blasingame in the third game. The Orange Crush did come alive as Denis Menke, Bob Watson, Jesus Alou, and Jimmy Wynn all had RBI doubles, and Watson and John Mayberry had home runs. The only problem was the Pirates also had an intimidating nickname: The Lumber Company, plus they were motivated by the return of manager Danny Murtaugh from medical leave,[2] allowing future Astros manager Bill Virdon to step down from the interim role.[3] The likes of Richie Hebner, Wilver Stargell (He and his family preferred his given name over "Willie." His family even enjoyed Vin Scully's Dodgers broadcasts most because he would use "Wilver."), Roberto Clemente, Manny Sanguillen, and Dave Cash did not let up. While Houston collected fifteen hits and eight runs, Pittsburgh had seventeen hits and nine runs.

It was simply a hitter's duel that someone, unfortunately, had to lose. The defeat added another one-run loss to the Astros' record, making that eleven this far in 1971.[4]

The road trip, which saw Houston sweep San Diego, split four with Cincinnati, and lose series to Atlanta and Pittsburgh, was now over, and they would be at the home sweet Dome for nine games, beginning June 8 with the Reds now visiting the Astros for two. The Reds were having somewhat similar struggles as the Orange Crush Astros in that they too were trying to start winning consistently rather than bounce around .500. The Big Red Machine, as the Reds were known, did not support their starting pitcher Gary Nolan, and Cesar Cedeno and Doug Rader each brought in a run, with the Red Rooster scoring John Mayberry on a triple. This game also saw the smallest crowd in the history of the Astrodome, with just 1,740 fans. The series was split the next day after Johnny Bench hit a solo home run off starter Jack Billingham and the Astros lost yet another game by one run.

The Braves followed for a four-game weekend beginning on Thursday, June 10. Dierker was pitching again, but the Braves' dangerous Hall of Fame duo in the middle of the lineup consisting of Hank Aaron and Orlando Cepeda roughed up the Houston starter early with an RBI triple and single, respectively. Dierker pitched scoreless ball after that, but the damage was done, and his hitters only gave him one run via Denis Menke single in the ninth, though they still had a winning threat that took Braves closer Cecil Upshaw to stave off and give the Astros a consecutive one-run loss. Atlanta's starter Tom Kelley had a no-hitter going into the seventh, but after Jimmy Wynn popped out to shortstop, Cesar Cedeno came up and noticed third baseman Earl Williams playing back. Cedeno thought he could bunt and get something started for his team, so he did, and the no-hitter was over.[5] Nowadays, this would be frowned upon due to unwritten rules, but in this case, Cedeno was simply trying to disrupt Kelley's rhythm.

Despite the loss, the fact that it took Dierker until the middle of June to experience two pitching losses was impressive. It is unclear if he switched out his shoes after this loss, or if/when he did at all in 1971.

Starter Wade Blasingame allowed three runs as the Braves tied the score in the ninth inning of Friday's game, but as they say, "The ball doesn't lie." In the bottom half of the inning, Jimmy Wynn and Johnny Edwards collected base hits, and with Wynn on third base and two outs, pinch-hitter Norm Miller hit a ground ball to shortstop Zoilo Versalles, prepared to flip to second but Marv Staehle was not at the bag, and Cesar Geronimo slid into second safely before Versalles could record the out. All meanwhile, Wynn touches home to win the game.[7] The "Secret Weapon" Norm Miller had come through once again.

That was a nickname Miller gave himself. As games went on, if it looked like he could be called upon to enter, he would begin hyping himself up in preparation to be the hero, even putting his jacket on like a cape. It tended to work for him, and he managed to have fun in spite of his skipper.[8]

Before Saturday's game, general manager Spec Richardson was on the field to honor Doug Rader for his Gold Glove award that he won for his defensive prowess in 1970. Rader became the first Houston player to win the award, though it would become his first of five in a row. It was also Cap Night in the Astrodome, with kids aged 14 and younger receiving free Astros caps upon entry.[6] It is unclear if the caps were the new orange ones, or if the promotion was devised to clear more of the old navy lids off the shelves.

Ken Forsch went the distance in a one-run game that went Houston's way, 3-2. Cedeno and Watson each singled in a run in the first frame, and Menke sacrificed another one two innings later after Watson led off the third with a triple. Don Wilson set out to win the series and build some excellent momentum for the Astros to end the series on the afternoon of Sunday, June 13. Instead, the Braves handed him his fourth loss and scored six runs to knock him out after two and two-thirds innings. The final score was 9-0, and it consisted of three home runs, two from

Earl Williams and the other from the usual suspect in the Atlanta lineup, Hammerin' Hank Aaron. The momentum was not built up, though the Astros could have really used it to begin the week, as they would welcome to town the Pirates, who were surging and were now in first place in the NL East and one game shy of the National League's best record. The Astros, on the other hand, dipped under .500 to 30-31 and nine games back of the league-leading Giants with the loss, though they were still in third place, three behind the Dodgers.

Game one of the series against Pittsburgh proved to be an exciting one, as well as one that proved the Astros still have the hunger as well as ability to win against premier teams. The Bucs struck first for two in the first inning, but a Jimmy Wynn double and Jack Billingham fielder's choice later, the game was tied at two in the fifth. An inning later, a Denis Menke sacrifice fly and Bob Watson home run put Houston in front by two. Dave Cash drove in two in their last chance in the top of the ninth, but their bullpen lacked control in the bottom half, and when Joe Morgan walked, Wynn scored the winning run.

Back to the mound came Larry Dierker, and the team and fans felt good about taking the series against a leading team in the league to put themselves back in postseason conversations. Through six and two/third innings, he put his team on his back and pitched scoreless ball and only allowed two hits. Unfortunately, his lineup provided no help, and after a while, something had to give. He allowed a solo home run to Al Oliver in the seventh inning, then three hits in the ninth, two of those being RBI singles. Jimmy Wynn reached second on a Steve Blass error in the bottom of the ninth, and Roger Metzger moved him to third with a base hit, but Norm Miller was not the superhero today, as with a strikeout looking, the Pirates evened the series. For the first time this season, Dierker suffered back-to-back losses.

Jimmy Wynn was written in the leadoff spot on the lineup card the next day, but that made no difference as Pittsburgh took the series 6-4. All four of Houston's runs came in the sixth inning as they nearly batted around: Wynn doubled, Morgan popped out, Cedeno doubled, Watson singled in both Wynn and Cedeno, Menke singled Watson to second, Edwards singled in Watson, Rader singled in Menke, Metzger grounded out. The Orange Crush was activated...for one inning. The Lumber Company was activated for three innings, enough time for them to score more than four runs. The Astros had an off day the next day, possibly with another morning workout with manager Walker, then it was off to the West Coast, where Don Wilson would start against the Dodgers.

Friday, June 18 was the day of another one-run loss, and Saturday was a fourth consecutive defeat, though by more than one run. The finale at Chavez Ravine was started by Dierker, who had his shortest outing of the season so far at one and one-third innings after giving up five runs in that span. Jim Ray took over after that, and the Orange Crush came out swinging to support the long reliever. Every run they scored came via single, and Doug Rader had three of them plus a double in a 4-for-5 day. The five runs scored in the third inning were all unearned since they came after Dodger third sacker Bobby Valentine threw away the possible third out and allowed Jack Hiatt to reach base.[9] The losing streak was over with an explosive day that favored the Orangemen 9-7, and now they got to take a day off, then visit San Diego on June 22 to continue their climb towards pennant contention.

Ken Forsch and Joe Morgan helped that cause by handing the Padres their seventh straight loss with, respectively, eight solid innings pitched and a three-RBI triple.[10] However, the Astros dropped the next two games along with the series in heartbreaking fashion, both in a doubleheader on June 23 and both lost by one run after walk-off hits in the twelfth and ninth innings, respectively. In game two of the twin-bill, Larry Dierker was brought on to record the last out of the eighth inning, but he surrendered an RBI single and was saddled with a blown save, a rarity for a starting pitcher.

The Astros headed home for the weekend after that, going from facing the last-place Padres to the first-place Giants. After losing two games in the last inning in San Diego, they won in the last inning in the first game against the Giants to beat Gaylord Perry on a wild pitch while Jack Hiatt was at bat, proceeded by Hiatt's RBI single over the shallow outfielders.[11] Interestingly, Hiatt still worked in the Giants' sales office during the offsea-

son.[12] With the high of the win going into June 26, Larry Dierker sought to get back on the winning side of the ledger. But just like his last start, one subpar inning that included a Bobby Bonds home run proved fatal for him, and his batters gave him only one run, meaning Dierker lost his fourth game. It is possible that it was during this stretch of losses for Dierker that he began experiencing some elbow pain. Forsch, who writers were beginning to compare to Dierker because of the similar size, delivery, and ability, went the distance and won his third consecutive start the next day to win the series for the Astros.

Veteran Jack Hiatt, former Giants catcher who still held a sales office job in San Francisco in 1971, maintained a batting average around .400 through the first half of the season.

Beating the league's toughest team would certainly give a ballclub confidence to beat another tough team, right? The Astros made it seem so when they won the next two games to clinch the series victory over the Braves, including Don Wilson's first win since June 8, which was decided by one run. The final game of June was lost by a single run, which was tough enough to get against Phil Niekro, but a Bob Watson home run in the game and a three-game winning streak before that had the team looking up. They only went 12-15 in the month which included three and four game losing streaks and a three-game winning streak, but several of the games they won were against teams in the running for the flag, such as the Pirates, Dodgers, and Giants. The Astros were twelve games out of first and two games under .500 at 37-39. Jack Hiatt's batting average had lowered to .367, but Cesar Cedeno was now batting .241, Bob Watson hitting .290, and Doug Rader, with a .229

average, had several stellar performances at the plate. Larry Dierker had his worst month of the season and his ERA had risen from 1.59 after his tenth win in Pittsburgh to 2.24 after his fourth loss against the Giants, but Ken Forsch helped by winning three games, two of them complete games.

In Ken Forch's first full big league season, he entered the starting rotation and won eight games, sparking comparisons to Larry Dierker in both performance and physical appearance.

QUIETLY PROVING THEMSELVES RIGHT

alf of the 1971 season was complete, and half was left to play. Both the last day of June and the first day of July were off days, but the Cincinnati Reds arrived at the Astrodome for four games on July 2, when Larry Dierker took the ball hoping to get off the schneid of three straight pitching losses. In an ideal way for the Astros to start the month, he did just that, winning a 3-2 affair in which the Toy Cannon Jimmy Wynn hit his third home run of the season off Gary Nolan, the same pitcher he hit his second off of back in May. Wynn's homer was his 175th career long ball, and it was retrieved in the left field bleachers by Tom Hunter from the suburb of Pearland. Eighteen years later in 1989, both Wynn and Hunter happened to be at Mile High Stadium in Denver, Colorado, on a day when an Old Timer's game was taking place. They met one another and Wynn personally signed the ball.[1]

Dierker allowed just two runs in eight and one/third innings, and closer Fred Gladding finished it up in the ninth with the help of Jack Hiatt catching Buddy Bradford attempting to steal. There was hope that both Dierker and Wynn were turning the tide and getting back to their usual selves, especially Wynn as he had been struggling all season to the point where he was not even regularly in the starting lineup.

July 3 saw Houston win another one-run game 4-3, but in thirteen innings. They scored three in the first, Cincinnati scored three in the ninth, and Jack Hiatt brought home Jimmy Wynn with a base hit in the thirteenth. Ken Forsch won his fourth straight in a 6-1 Independence Day Orange Crush onslaught. Denis Menke and Bob Watson each singled in a run, Hiatt sacrificed in two, and Joe Morgan put a Tony Cloninger pitch over the deep outfield wall in the seventh for a solo shot. In addition to celebrating the United States of America's independence on July 4, the Astros were hosting their annual Corpus Christi Day for fans from the smaller city in south Texas.[2] The series had been won by the Space City, and they swept it the next day by winning another game 4-3 after a sons and daughters promotional game.

Two days after Larry Dierker got back on the winning side of the ledger, he won the hearts of the Corpus Christi Sparklettes on the Fourth of July.

The Astros were heating up in the hottest month of the year, exactly what they needed headed into San Francisco on Tuesday, July 6. The Astros were now over .500 after the four-game sweep of the Reds, and nine games away from the Giants, who were now a half-game back of the Pirates for the best record in the league. A three-run first inning consisting of run-scoring singles from Bob Watson and Jimmy Wynn made the difference in a 5-2 Astros win in the first game of three at Candlestick Park. The Orange Crush was present the next day in a big way to support their ace. They batted around in both the fourth and sixth innings, scoring ten and six runs in each of those innings, respectively. Cesar Cedeno went three-for-six with four RBI and two runs scored. The Bull was 3-for-5 with three RBI and a run scored. The Toy Cannon, who was batting in the bottom half of the order by now, was 2-for-3 with two RBI and two runs scored, including a seventh inning double for his one thousandth career hit. The Red Rooster only got one hit in four tries, but he touched home three times. Even Larry Dierker brought in a run and scored one. Final score: 18-4, a franchise record at the time for most runs scored.[3] The all-

The only thing that could stand in ace pitcher Larry Dierker's way of a record season in 1971 was elbow pain, and during a cold and windy San Francisco game in early July, that is what spelled the beginning of the end of his campaign, though he still mustered the five innings needed to earn the win.

around dominating win was the Astros' sixth in a row, and they were now down to seven games out of first place.

However, not all Astros news on July 7 was good news. While Dierker won his twelfth game, the Bay Area weather was not the most pleasant for this Wednesday game, and this did not help Dierker's already-ailing arm. In previous starts, he had begun to feel some discomfort, but since he felt it did not affect his pitching, he did not pay much attention to it. He figured that perhaps that meant he was throwing his slider correctly and his arm just needed to adjust to it. But on this day, his pain became severe, and it did affect his pitching. He threw five innings of eight-hit, four-run ball before Jim Ray came on to record the four-inning save. Since the All Star Game was nearing, there was speculation that Dierker would be selected to start the game on the mound for the National League.[4] Unfortunately, when he received the invitation to play in the game, he could not play due to his arm trouble.[5]

Outfielder Jay Schlueter only appeared in one Major League season, the 1971 Astros season, and only in seven games, all but one in July, but mustered one hit in three at-bats for a career .333 batting average.

His eventual replacement in the Midsummer Classic, Don Wilson, got the ball for the Astros the next day as they tried for a second consecutive sweep, this one against the cream of the division. Wilson pitched the whole game but struggled, allowing four runs on six hits in a 4-2 loss. However, Doug Rader hit a solo homer in the fourth inning, and they had still won the series, their fourth straight winning series.

That changed when the team arrived in St. Louis. A scheduled doubleheader the night of Friday, July 9, saw Steve Carlton beat Ken Forsch for his first loss in over a month, and then a high-scoring game that saw the Red Rooster and the Toy Cannon both go deep, though Houston's five runs were no match for St. Louis' nine, four of those coming off two Julian Javier triples. Outfielder Jay Schlueter, who made his big league debut on June 18 in Los Angeles, collected his first hit in the fifth inning of the second game. Both teams combined for 31 hits on July 10, so the Orange

Crush was still on, but it was the Cardinals who scraped away with the win, walking it off with a double in the ninth that scored future Astros legend Jose Cruz. Reliever Jim Ray started on the mound for the Astros in the fourth and final game of the series, and Bob Gibson took the bump for the Cardinals as the Cards swept the Astros going into the All Star break, though they did muster three runs in the eighth with the help of a Cesar Cedeno home run, and six hits overall. Both Don Wilson and Ken Forsch came out of the bullpen after Ray lasted four and one/third innings.

Other Astros on the All Star ballot were Joe Morgan for second base, Denis Menke for shortstop, Doug Rader for third base, and Jimmy Wynn for outfield. Both Cesar Cedeno and Bob Watson were outfielders (Part-time in Watson's case) that were having a better season than Wynn, so that decision to have Wynn on the ballot was likely one made from reputation rather than that season's performance. Guys that the organization had traded in years past that were on the ballot were Rusty Staub, Jerry Grote, and Sandy Alomar.[6] As for players who made the All Star rosters, Staub and Mike Cuellar were former Astros that went on to fulfill their potential away from Houston. The players that did represent the Astros were Larry Dierker and Don Wilson, though Dierker was injured, leaving only Wilson to play in the big game on the night of July 13 at venerable Tiger Stadium in Detroit.

Wilson entered the game in the seventh inning in succession of Dock Ellis, Juan Marichal, and Fergie Jenkins. He pitched both the seventh and eighth innings and was a walk short of perfection. He got the Royals' Amos Otis to fly out to left, Cookie Rojas to fly out to right, and the Orioles' Don Buford to strikeout swinging in the seventh. In the eighth, the Red Sox' Carl Yastrzemski walked, the hometown Tigers' Al Kaline struck out swinging, and the Twins' Harmon Killebrew grounded into a double play, fielded by the Cubs' Ron Santo and third, thrown to the Braves' Felix Millan at second, and then onto the Red's Lee May at first to retire Yaz, Killebrew, and the side. Houston was surely disappointed that they only had one player representing them, but they were also excited that their guy showed out on the national stage.

Wilson dodged a bullet in this game as every run was scored via a home run, and there were lots of them. Reds' Johnny Bench in the third inning, Braves' Hank Aaron in the top of the third, A's Reggie Jackson and Orioles' Frank Robinson in the bottom half, Harmon Killebrew in the sixth, and Pirates' Roberto Clemente in the eighth. Jackson's was the most spectacular of them all, hitting a transformer on the roof over the right/center field grandstand. The 1971 All Star Game is often considered a display of future Hall of Famers as 22 players who were on either roster later were inducted into the National Baseball Hall of Fame.

Don Wilson was the lone Houston All Star representative, and he put up the best pitching line of the four pitchers in the game, striking out two in two innings of near-perfect ball.

The days off did not help the Astros right away once they got back to the Astrodome for their 1971 season schedule on July 15. Ken Forsch lost his second start in a row, 9-4, extending the losing streak to six, the longest losing skid the Astros would have in 1971. Despite Joe Morgan, Cesar Cedeno, Johnny Edwards, and Roger Metzger bringing in four runs in the first two innings, the Mets chipped away and eventually totaled nine runs, three of them coming off of a Cleon Jones three-run home run to right field over another banner that said "BEAT THE METS ORANGE CRUSH."[7] The Astros obeyed the sign the next day as they built up an eventual nine-run output to top both Nolan Ryan and the Mets' four runs.

It was during this game on July 16 that the Astros turned the first triple play in franchise history. In the top of the third, with Ken Boswell on second and Tommie Agee on first, Cleon Jones hit to Roger Metzger at shortstop, who stepped on second to putout Agee and threw to Denis Menke at first base to get Jones out. Boswell started running toward third base late, and Menke noticed and threw to Doug Rader, who tagged Boswell out, and the side was put out all in one batted ball.[8]

Earlier in the contest, Jimmy Wynn was at-bat in the first inning against Nolan Ryan, who had walked the bases loaded prior to Wynn stepping up. With a 3-0 count, he ignored the "take" sign and swung and popped out. An alleged blowup between Wynn and manager Harry Walker ensued in the clubhouse, and ultimately Wynn was fined $100.[9] The Toy Cannon threatened Houston Chronicle writer John Wilson, the same writer who had given Wynn his nickname, that if the incident showed up in the paper the next day, Wilson would be beaten up. Wilson said it would, and Wynn told him that he would attack him if he ever showed up in the clubhouse again.[10]

With Tom Seaver and Larry Dierker on the mound to finish the series, Houston swarmed the Astrodome for the highest home attendance the Astros had in 1971 at 32,852 spectators. While fans were not at a premium, scoring was, given that two of the top National League pitchers were starting this game, though Dierker left after just three and two-thirds innings. Ken Boswell singled in Seaver in the third, and Doug Rader responded in the fifth with a game-tying home run. In the bottom of the ninth, Roger Metzger cracked a base hit to center, Joe Morgan bunted him over, and the Mets intentionally walked Wynn to set up the double play and avoid the power threat. Cesar Cedeno made them pay, however, as he put a single into right field that the second baseman Boswell could not handle and Metzger scored the winning run. The Astros had won another series.

In an unusual scheduling sequence, the following day, Sunday, July 18, the Phillies came to town for a doubleheader plus an additional game on Monday before parting ways. Jekyll and Hyde would have liked this doubleheader, with the first game being a 1-0 pitcher's duel between Ken Reynolds and Don Wilson that the Phillies won, and the second game a 10-7 hitting festival that the Orange Crush won. Starter Wade Blasingame hit a two-RBI double, Doug Rader scored two runs with a triple, and Jimmy Wynn hit his fifth home run of the year into deep left field.

The Monday game went eleven innings, of which Phillies starter Rick Wise, another All Star, pitched ten of, and Astros rookie Bill Greif pitched six and one/third of. The top of the seventh inning saw Tim McCarver commit interference against Houston shortstop Roger Metzger, resulting in two outs. Phillies skipper Frank Lucchesi and coach George Myatt were both ejected by second base umpire Bruce Froemming for using profanity during the ensuing argument.[11] In the last frame, Roger Metzger, Joe Morgan, and Jimmy Wynn all reached base on a base hit, error, and intentional walk, respectively. With one strike on him, Cesar Cedeno grounded a single through the left side of the infield, scoring Metzger to win 3-2 and take a one-run game in a hard-fought effort.

*As soon as Cesar Cedeno reached the big leagues in 1970,
the young star center fielder began to prove himself as a five-tool
player, and he carried it over in 1971.*

The next three days were colorful, as the Astros' Orange Crush uniforms were joined in the Dome by the powder blue uniforms and tri-colored caps of the Montreal Expos for the second time in 1971. The Canadians had swept a three-game set in Houston in April, and the two teams split two games north of the border in early May, so the Astros were looking to set the record straight that they were a premier team that could easily beat a lowly team like the Expos. They also wanted to gain ground on the Giants with some easy wins. The adage in baseball, after all, is that "you can't win pennants by splitting with the second-division clubs. You must build your lead on the tailenders."[12] Since the Expos were in last place in the NL Eastern division, now was the time to do just that.

It didn't happen to start the series on July 20, two years to the day after the NASA Johnson Space Center just 27 miles from the Astrodome guided Apollo 11 onto the Moon's surface. Ken Forsch lasted an inning and one/third, and his team was held scoreless until the bottom of the ninth, when they put three on the board, just enough to tie the game and allow Montreal to get a run in the top of the tenth with no response in the bottom half. 4-3, another one-run defeat. Jack Billingham gave a better starting effort the next day in eight innings, but the Expos clinched the series with a 5-3 win with the help of a Joe Morgan error in the top of the ninth that allowed two unearned runs that put the Expos in front.[13] In the sixth inning with Cesar Cedeno at the plate, Jimmy Wynn stole home. He had previously done so in 1965, so this was not a one-off event for him.[14] After all, speed does not slump in baseball, and Wynn still had plenty of that in 1971.

With Wade Blasingame pitching to finish the three-game set with the foreign team, the Orange Crush scored eight runs. A bases-loaded walk and a double plated four in the first, and three RBI hits in the eighth—a Doug Rader base hit, a Denis Menke double, and an RBI single by relief pitcher George Culver of all people—doubled the score, adding up to an Astros win of 8-2. Joe Morgan scored once and collected two doubles and two walks in the game. The Thursday getaway day victory kept the Astros alive for a chance at an even 6-6 split in the season series with the Expos.

Pitcher George Culver was on his fourth MLB team during his time in Houston, which consisted of two and a half seasons of solid relief.

Back to Hobby Airport to begin a road trip that would take the Astros into August. They headed to the Northeast to visit the homes of the same three teams they had just played in the Dome, and in the same order. Therefore, Shea Stadium in New York on July 23 was the first stop. Don Wilson picked up his first win after his All Star Game appearance in a three-hit, one-run complete game over Nolan Ryan that saw Jimmy Wynn go deep to begin the scoring in the third inning. The Mets put up crooked numbers in three different innings to beat Bill Greif, who faced four batters and gave up three runs before the bullpen was called, by a score of 9-3 on July 24, then two crooked numbers the next day to run Ken Forsch out in the fourth inning and win the series with a 7-6 victory, though the Orange Crush did come out in force with home runs off the bats of Joe Morgan and Norm Miller.

The team hoped better fortunes would find them at Veterans Stadium in Philadelphia. They did not find fortunes in the first game of four to start the week, because they had to work for a win. A fifteen-inning game on July 26 saw the Phillies open with a solo homer in the first, Jesus Alou cut the deficit in half with a double in the fifth, Cesar Cedeno tie it with a double in the eighth, Cedeno give his team the lead with another double followed by a Doug Rader RBI single in the tenth, George Culver blow the save in the bottom of the tenth by allowing the Phils to tie the game, then Rader and Alou each hit RBI doubles to plate three runs and give Jim Ray the pitching win. Ray had not pitched since July 20 due to an ankle sprain, but he had it taped up and he retired twelve straight batters upon entering this game, giving him his seventh win of 1971.[15] The game went four hours and twelve minutes, the longest game the Astros had played so far, but they kept themselves in it for a solid win.[16]

On July 27, the Astros and Phillies played a doubleheader, the first game making up a rained-out contest from May 8. In the makeup, Larry Dierker, once the infallible pitching ace of the team, struggled once again, surrendering seven runs on nine hits and four home runs, two being back-to-back in the first inning and the other two both coming from Bobby

Pfeil, in six and one/third innings. RBI hits by Cedeno and Rader were not enough to help that, and Dierker was saddled with his fifth loss.

The regularly scheduled game went much better as Wade Blasingame went the distance and held the opposition to one run on four hits. Jimmy Wynn, having been batting third in the lineup more often by now, hit an opposite field single with two out in the first, stole second and advanced to third on a throwing error before Cedeno stayed hot at the plate with a towering shot into left field to give his club an early 2-0 lead. If Doug Rader doing the same in the seventh inning was not enough, Denis Menke and Jesus Alou brought in a run apiece in the ninth to win 5-1. Both Cedeno and Rader collected four hits and scored two runs on the day.

To win the series, Walker sent Don Wilson to the mound, and except for a three-run seventh inning, he pitched a great game, going all nine and giving up six hits, three of which came in that seventh inning. That gave Wilson the support he needed, as Cedeno and Jesus Alou each doubled, Roger Metzger and Joe Morgan each tripled, and Metzger also stole a bag. The coming off day after the 6-3 win would feel good.

The last destination before heading home was abroad, to Jarry Park (Or Parc Jarry, in Canada) in Montreal, for four games as there was another twin-bill necessary to make up another rained-out game from May 4. That would happen on July 30, a date on which two year earlier in New York, the Astros dominated the Mets by beating Nolan Ryan, Fred Gladding getting his only career hit, Jimmy Wynn and Denis Menke each hitting grand slams in the same inning, and Larry Dierker hitting a home run in a doubleheader.

Unfortunately, despite homers by Jesus Alou in the second inning and Doug Rader in the seventh for a birthday homer, the Expos took the makeup game 7-4, clinching a winning record against Houston for 1971 and handing Ken Forsch another loss, his fourth consecutive. The second game was tough for the Astros, but in ten innings they got it done to give Jim Ray an 8-2 record, astounding for a reliever who is not the regular closer. In the fourth inning of that game, Jesus Alou broke the scoring open for Houston by doubling in Rich Chiles who started in left field, then Larry Howard, who got the start at catcher, hit a three-run home run to tie the game at four. Off Mike Marshall in the tenth, Alou singled in Cesar Geronimo, who had come on for Chiles in the seventh, and that run was all that was needed for a 6-5 victory.

Chiles and Howard started again on the last day of July, and Chiles brought in Joe Morgan, who homered earlier in the game, with a late-inning double. But that, along with a Jesus Alou long ball, could not overcome Jack Billingham giving up five runs on six hits in four and two-thirds innings. There was still one more game to play on August 1, but at the end of July, the Astros were 53-53, exactly at .500, eleven games back of the first-place Giants, but now the Braves had overtaken Houston for third place by two games. It seemed that anything good was not staying that way long enough for it to propel the team back into the pennant race, but those good things showed up in July perhaps more than any other month.

Other outfielders were still in front of Rich Chiles on the depth chart in 1971, but he maintained reliable stats and seemed to come through for the Astros when he did play.

After Cedeno started 1971 cold, batting .176 when manager Walker decided to bench him, Cedeno had returned to the lineup when Jimmy Wynn was having a back problem. Since them, the Dominican star batted over .300 to raise his season batting average to .262.[17] Doug Rader was up to .253 and seven home runs, and Jesus Alou was maintaining his average above .300, with his number being at .314 at the close of the month. Alou also hit two home runs in the last two days, though those are the only two times he would do so in 1971. Bob Watson, who had not played since July 16 due to military service, was stuck at five home runs, but his average was at .293.[18] Jack Hiatt saw his average lower to a still fine .283.

Rough months from Larry Dierker and Ken Forsch were partly made up by the All Star appearance and slight resurgence of Don Wilson, who won two games to end July. Jim Ray was also having a career year out of the bullpen with an 8-2 record and 2.15 ERA, and George Culver was having his best season he would have as an Astro with a 2.40 ERA. Fred Gladding, the closer, did not have as good a record as Ray, but his ERA was lower at 1.59.

There were two months left in the season that had so much hype in Houston at the beginning of it, but now many people were counting them out. However, they had just gone 16-14 during the month of July, and many of their wins happened to come when the Giants also won. The pieces were still here, so all they needed to do was come together to further prepare themselves for the stretch run.

AUGUST

WRONG PLACE AT THE WRONG TIME

Finishing up the road trip in Montreal to start August, starting pitcher Wade Blasingame allowed ten hits, but the Expos only scored one run, which is less than the amount of RBI Blasingame had. He extended a 3-1 Houston lead with a two-RBI double to make the score 5-1 in the seventh inning, two frames before both the Toy Cannon and the Red Rooster tattooed Jim Britton pitches out of Jarry Park. As Wynn's homer brought in Joe Morgan, the score became 8-1, and that is how the Orange Crush achieved an August 1 win. Now they got to head back to Dome Sweet Dome, where they were 30-24 so far.

On August 2 and 3, the Cubs would come to Houston for two games that writers deemed to be a very important series for the Astros if they wanted to climb up in the NL West standings. The Baytown Sun put it this way: "If ever the Orangemen had an important series, and if ever they needed to make a move, this is it." In Houston's favor was that the first-place Giants, as well as the contending Dodgers, Braves, and Reds, were faltering as of late, the Astros were finished with the Expos for the season, and the Cubs were a team that did not like playing in the Astrodome, partly because of their struggles there.[1]

Back in 1966, Cubs manager Leo Durocher went as far to say about the Eighth Wonder of the World that it was a "$45 million stadium with a 10-cent infield," as well as calling the Astros a "bush organization." The next time his club went to the Dome, as his team surrendered a comfortable lead in the ninth to lose in walk off fashion, Durocher responded to a taunt on the scoreboard by ripping a bullpen phone off the dugout wall and throwing it onto the field. Plate umpire Tony Venzon placed the phone back in the dugout, and the scoreboard announced that Durocher would be billed for the damage, which he was.[2]

The luxurious Astrodome was the Eighth Wonder of the World for fans and for Astros players, but for the Chicago Cubs, it was a house of horrors where their struggles seemed to show more than usual.

The schedule turning to August, along with a vital homestand beginning, gave the Astros a lift that, after an exhibition girls' softball game between Texas state championship teams, helped Don Wilson throw a two-hitter and beat Fergie Jenkins in a 2-1 pitcher's duel.[3]

The second game of the series was "Straight A Night," when students with straight A's were guests of the organization and the Houston Chronicle. This contest was also a hurler's duel between Bill Hands and Larry Dierker, but Dierker, with only a Ron Santo solo home run as a flaw, was replaced by Jim Ray in the seventh inning with the Cubs leading 1-0. The Orange Crush had their chances, including after a pinch-hit Norm Miller single and Joe Morgan double in the eighth that put runners on second and third, but nothing came of it. Fred Gladding's four-run giveaway in the ninth inning only further solidified a Cubs victory and Dierker's sixth loss.

At least the Astros worked out a split with the Cubs, and now they were to play two versus the Dodgers, whom the Astros had done well against to this point. Facing tough National League opponents was what would get Houston back into the thick of the race, and it was also where they tended to succeed the most. Lesser teams, namely the Expos, tended to give the Astros the most fits. So, if the Cubs duo of games was not critical enough, now these two are against a divisional opponent whom they were three-and-a-half games back of, while ten-and-a-half games out of first.

There were thirteen combined hits on August 4–four from the Dodgers and nine from the Astros–but Cesar Cedeno provided the only scoring when he cracked a base hit into center field that scored Roger Metzger and Joe Morgan and allowed Cedeno to make it to second base, though he was promptly picked off. That was all Ken Forsch needed to break his four-game losing streak and earn his sixth win, over the team that almost drafted him out of Oregon State University back in 1968.[4]

If Houston could rally behind Jack Billingham and sweep the pair of contests against Los Angeles, they would climb up in the standings. A common problem they had in 1971 was that anytime they would win, it was followed by a loss that cancelled out the win, and/or a team that they needed to gain ground on would also have won. Fortunately, when Houston lost, those other teams typically lost as well, but this meant that much of 1971 was spent in stalemate waiting for something to turn the table so a true upward path could guide them into the pennant race.

The trend only continued on August 5, Youth Baseball Night, when Bill Singer shut out the Astros 3-0 despite the Dodgers collecting no extra-base hits. They got seven singles, two of them brought in runs, and the third run came courtesy of a sacrifice fly. That is how the Dodgers won most of the time during this era: get a runner on, move him over in whatever menial way they can, find a way to have him touch home plate, then let the pitching do their thing. It was "small ball" at its finest. The Astros were just as capable of this style of play as that is the kind of play that former general manager Paul Richards envisioned when he was with the organization, though they had the additional advantage of power, which adds an element of surprise to small ball when the other team never knows when someone may put a ball into the gap, down the line, or into the bleachers.

The scoreless game for the Astros in one of the two games in each two-game series this week, and the fact that in the games they won, they scored all their runs in one inning, meant that going into the weekend, they had scored in only two of their last 34 innings.[5]

Also on August 5, Norm Miller had his season cut short due to injury.

With two outs in the bottom of the seventh, possibly after wandering the dugout with his jacket cape on, Miller pinch-hit for relief pitcher George Culver. Miller hit a line drive that hit off the shin of Dodgers pitcher Singer and ricocheted to first baseman Dick Allen, whom the Dodgers had acquired before the season from the Cardinals. Miller collided with Allen as he was running towards first base, and this broke Miller's wrist. He was not placed on the disabled list, but he did not play again in 1971. It is unclear if Miller had lightning bolts painted on his shoes when this incident occurred, since he painted those on until the clubhouse attendant was told to polish the décor off.[6]

Norm Miller's 1971 campaign, one which was already frustrating for him as he saw his playing time decrease for unknown reasons, ended in injury in early August.

Beginning on August 6, the Padres played three weekend games in Houston, a good chance for the Astros to gain the ground they were not able to earlier in the week, especially considering that Bob Watson was back.[7] That day in particular saw the Miss Astro pageant contestants introduced and the popular Nickel Beer Night. The Padres overshadowed a Doug Rader home run and another Wade Blasingame RBI (Something he did abnormally well for a pitcher) with four runs and a save, coincidentally for Nickel Beer Night, by Bob Miller. Once the game ended, drunk fans raided the field and visiting dugout, and it took police to stop the chaos.[8] The next day, after fans received photo buttons upon entry, Don Wilson got the support of Rich Chiles, who tied the game in the sixth with a single and set his teammates up to take the lead and even the series at one apiece, setting up a Sunday afternoon rubber match with Larry Dierker starting. Dierker gave up one run on two hits in just one inning before Denny Lemaster replaced him and ultimately took the loss thanks to a two-run fourth inning highlighted by a Nate Colbert home run to lead off the fourth inning. Before the game, Anita Waller-Ney of El Paso, Texas, was crowned Miss Astro in the Miss Astro pageant.[9]

A growing story surrounding the ballclub was that Jimmy Wynn reportedly wanted out of Houston. General manager Spec Richardson brushed off Wynn's wishes, saying that most baseball players, including Wynn, express desire to be traded every year but do not always mean it. Wynn's patience for manager Harry Walker was virtually gone by this point, as for a little over three years now Walker freely dispersed his reign of terror on the Astros clubhouse, especially those members of it that were not white. Wynn added that his top two trade destinations would be New York or Los Angeles.[10] Wynn later denied asking for a trade and simply mentioned New York and Los Angeles as places he would want to be traded should he be.[11]

Injuries were also beginning to plague the Astros. After Larry Dierker's very short start versus the Padres, he did not pitch again during the 1971 season. After a fantastic start, his elbow pain was now too much for him to continue. Catcher Johnny Edwards had been hurt for over a week, and two other guys who could catch, Marty Martinez and Norm Miller, were dealing with hand issues, leaving Jack Hiatt as the sole catcher. Roger Metzger was complaining about a sore back, and he also left Sunday's game early in the fourth inning.[12] This was not at all the start to August that manager Walker needed just as the team had opportunities to get back into the thick of the race.

An off day gave the team time to recuperate and begin a long road trip that would keep them away from the Dome until August 23. They first arrived in Cincinnati for two games, who along with San Diego, were the only two NL West teams behind the Astros in the standings. Just as they had done most of the season, every series during this trip was split except for one. The Astros split two against the Reds, split four in Atlanta, lost two of three in Pittsburgh, and split four in Chicago, meaning the Astros gained no ground. By the time the Cardinals awaited them in Houston, the Astros had lost a game-and-a-half to the Giants.

Roger Metzger was lauded for his ability in Spring Training in 1971, and he showed why during the season, providing valuable speed and defense when Denis Menke played first base.

However, there were some highlights of the journey. Joe Morgan homered to tie him with Doug Rader for the team home run lead with nine, and to help Ken Forsch to a win against the Reds on August 10. It was the next day that Gary Nolan got revenge on the team that had Forsch, Don Wilson, and Larry Dierker each beat him in games earlier in the season by just one run.[13]

In Atlanta, Johnny Edwards joined the lineup again and the Astros scored five runs in the first game on August 12. That would have been great if the Braves had not scored that many in the first inning alone, plus five more over the course of the game thanks to two long balls by eventual Rookie of the Year Earl Williams. The next day, the Orange Crush knocked around Hall of Famer Phil Niekro with two long balls, one from Cesar Cedeno in the third that scored three runs and one from Joe Morgan in the seventh that plated two. Bob Watson tripled after Cedeno's blast and was later brought in by Doug Rader's base hit. All of this backed up Don Wilson's complete game and eleventh win. The tide turned on

Saturday, August 14, when Pat Jarvis, who was 14-2 in his career against the Astros going into this game, pitched a three-hitter to shut out the orange men for the third time in 1971.[14] Larry Dierker was a probable starter for this game, but Ron Cook was given the ball.

Harry Walker injured a hamstring while playing in the Old Timer's Game before the last game of the series in Atlanta, but he surely felt better after the team was not fazed by Ken Forsch's struggle highlighted by deep home runs from Hammerin' Hank Aaron and Earl Williams. On the same day that President Richard Nixon announced the elimination of the gold standard for U.S. currency, the orange team struck gold with an early Doug Rader two-run homer and a Jimmy Wynn two-run single in the eighth that gave Houston the lead, and Forsch a tough win. The papers were saying that Wynn wanted to be traded, but he really wanted to return

The 1971 Astros were young but had a few veterans, and catcher Johnny Edwards was one of them who provided valuable leadership in the clubhouse and for the pitching staff, as well as great defense behind the plate.

to his Toy Cannon form that the league grew accustomed to in years prior. The go-ahead base hit in this game restored some of his confidence, at least for an afternoon.[15]

Three Rivers Stadium is where the Astros headed next to begin the work week on August 16. Doug Rader's eleventh home run was not enough to take down the Bucs as former Astro Dave Giusti earned a two-inning save, a feat Houston likely would have seen from him more often had Spec Richardson not included him in the deal to acquire Johnny Edwards. Don Wilson struggled on hump day and Denny Lemaster also lost when

Milt May hit a walk-off single and gave the Astros another one-run loss, but in between these two losses came a one-run win. Things looked bleak for most of that game, which was easy to see when Roberto Clemente hit both a home run and RBI single in the same game and the team was down 4-1 going into the late innings. But the oranges were picked in the seventh inning as Jimmy Wynn led off with a walk, then scored on a Denis Menke single. Jesus Alou and Cesar Cedeno brought in runs with hits, with an error by glove master Bill Mazeroski trying to turn a double play in between those two hits, and Doug Rader sacrificed in another run for a five-run inning, which carried the Orange Crush through the ninth and into the win column. Astros radio broadcaster Loel Passe remarked his belief that "We aren't out of the National League race by a long shot."[16]

To keep that true, the Astros would have to win more than they lost, not win as many as they lost. They got that chance with four games in three days at Wrigley Field, with the first two games being part of a doubleheader to make up an April 21 game that was rained out. The Astros did not initially take advantage of this chance as they were swept in the twin bill. In game one, Fergie Jenkins achieved his twentieth win in a complete game, solidifying his fifth straight twenty-win campaign. All the scoring happened in the first two innings; Cesar Cedeno and Rich Chiles brought in a run each in the top of the first, and the Cubs scored three in the bottom of the second. From there, pitching took over to keep the one-run differential, leaving the Astros with another loss by a single run. Ron Cook started for Houston, but if Larry Dierker had been healthy all season, this game possibly could have been the top game of the day in baseball, with two aces on the mound looking to be the first National League pitcher to reach twenty wins in 1971.

The second game was also a one-run loss, this time by a score of 5-4, but the Orange Crush still made an appearance. Doug Rader plated two runs in the third inning with a base hit to right field. Starting pitcher Ken Forsch brought in one with a single in the fourth, which knocked Cubs starter Ken Holtzman out of the ballgame. Joe Morgan responded to Billy Williams' fourth inning home run with a blast of his own in the fifth.

On the mound, Forsch gave up three runs in over six innings, but it was George Culver who, after holding the score in the seventh, blew the save in the eighth when J.C. Martin hit a two-RBI double. Three straight losses.

The next two days saw the Orange Crush make up for the double-header loss, first with a 3-0 win on August 21. The orange attack came in the third inning, starting with a Jack Hiatt home run to lead off the inning, a Roger Metzger triple, and two outs later, Joe Morgan traded places with Metzger. Rich Chiles scored Cesar Cedeno in the ninth to give Jack Billingham a little more comfort to finish his complete-game victory.

Bob Watson, first baseman as well as left fielder and former catcher, lived up to his nickname "Bull" in 1971 by being one of the most consistent and reliable hitters in the lineup, even after returning from military duty mid-season.

August 22, the final day of the long road trip, was won by one, 4-3. Jim Ray won his ninth game by coming on to get his team out of a bases-loaded jam in the seventh, then continuing to pitch flawless ball the rest of the way. The Bull, Bob Watson, went 3-for-5 with two singles, one of them bringing in a run in the first, and a fifth-inning long ball. The Little General, Joe Morgan and the Red Rooster, Doug Rader, each had only one hit, but they were doubles, and Rader came around to score after his to make up for an uncharacteristic second-inning error that resulted in an unearned run. The long, nearly two-week trip was now over, and since there were an odd number of games at thirteen, that means that they could not split those games, but the Astros came as close as you can, winning six and losing seven. Three of those losses were only by one run. However, the Orange Crush had two solid wins against the Cubs to ride momentum from going back to the Astrodome to face the Redbirds.

That did not seem to help much as Bob Gibson led the Cardinals to victory with an RBI single in the ninth to score Jose Cruz in the first of three games, handing Don Wilson his first loss since July 18 even though the Astros outhit the Cards seven to six. August 24, back-to-school night for the kids, who were given team rulers, pencils, and notepads, was not any better.[17] Ken Forsch pitched eight innings of two-run ball, one of which was unearned, but other than a last-minute base hit in the ninth from Rich Chiles to score Cesar Cedeno, the Astros were shut out. Defensively, Jesus Alou and Joe Morgan teamed up for a successful relay in gunning down Joe Torre trying for a triple to end the top of the first inning. A run still scored on the play, and the Astros had now lost 35 of 62 one-run ballgames in 1971, with the winning Cardinals run coming after Lou Brock stole third base then came home after Johnny Edwards' throw went into the outfield. With the lineup not producing enough runs to make a difference in close games, pitchers felt more pressure to not make mistakes, which leads to more mistakes. Every game became bigger and bigger as the team stayed where they were in the standings and with around the same number of games behind first place, but with fewer and fewer games left to play with every passing day.[18]

When the Astros tried to salvage one game from the Cardinals on August 25, Doug Rader kept them in the game with a solo shot to deep left field, his twelfth homer of the season, but St. Louis catcher Ted Simmons did the same in the eighth inning off George Culver, with a runner on base. Additionally, Rader was ejected in the eighth inning after arguing too much with home plate umpire John McSherry, who made his MLB debut back on June 1 in a game that the Astros were playing in Atlanta. This was McSherry's first ejection at the Major League level. By a score of 4-1, Houston was swept, with the dangerous Lumber Company Pirates strolling in next.[19]

Thursday, August 26 was an off day so the football Houston Oilers and Dallas Cowboys could play a game in the Astrodome that night for the "Governor's Cup," which the Cowboys won. The first 5,000 kids that entered the Dome on Friday, August 27 received a Pirates button, since that was the Astros' opponent. Roberto Clemente went 3-for-5 to extend the Astros' losing streak to four, but Don Wilson helped keep it at four the next night with a complete-game five-hit shutout of the NL East leaders. Four runs, two in the third inning and two in the fifth and Bob Watson responsible for one of those in each inning, provided the scoring for the Orange Crush. Before Saturday night's game, an Old Timer's Game was held, showcasing former decorated big league stars such as Bill Dickey, Johnny Mize, Carl Erskine, Stan Musial, Joe DiMaggio, and former Astro Don Nottebart.[20]

For the first time since the Astros played the Pirates in Pittsburgh a week and a half earlier and the first time under the Dome since August 8, before the long road trip, the S'tros would get to play in a rubber match to try to win a series. Pirates starter Bob Johnson gave up two runs on a Bob Watson ninth inning single, but before that, Wade Blasingame, Jim Ray, and George Culver combined to surrender five. Dave Giusti, like he did in the first game, got the save against his former employer, his 27th of the season, and that sealed the deal on a 4-8 season against the Bucs. If the Astros were to make a stretch drive in the last month of the season and win the NL West, the prospect of playing the Pirates in the National League Championship Series would not have looked good for this bunch.

Harry Walker called a closed-door clubhouse meeting after this game to focus his team on winning ballgames more than "bellyaching" and complaining, particularly to the writers.[21] This is the same team that started hot in the beginning of April, hot enough to be in first place and earn a nickname, and that as recently as August 7 were in third place and eight-and-a-half games behind the Giants. To end the month, they would now be in fifth place, seven games under .500, and fifteen games back after losing the first two games in a four-game Dome series that went into September.

The first game against the Dodgers was on August 30, the night honoring both Bob Watson and Roger Metzger with giveaway portraits.[22] The game was lost, as typical for the Astros in 1971, by one run, 3-2, with Cesar Cedeno's RBI double being the high point of the night. However, there were fireworks in a different way. In just the first inning, Dodger left fielder Willie Crawford got the suspicion that Ken Forsch was throwing at him on purpose. Astros catcher Jack Hiatt got in front of Crawford to keep him from yelling at the pitcher, which resulted in more tension and, soon thereafter, physical violence and the dugouts emptying. Hiatt got

two good licks on Crawford before Doug Rader got to him and pinned him to the AstroTurf. Rader ended up with cleat marks all over his back, some of which were from closer Fred Gladding, who ran onto the field without his trademark glasses on.

Both Hiatt and Crawford were ejected, though Hiatt probably would have left anyways as his nose was broken, and the game was relatively calm after that, as were the Astros' bats in the last game of the month the next day. Nine hits produced only one run as Doyle Alexander went the distance for Los Angeles. Rich Chiles singled in Cesar Cedeno in the fourth, but by then three Dodger runs had been scored in the first inning, and three more were to follow. Ron Cook took

Jack Hiatt's stellar hitting season was interrupted by his nose being broken in a fight with the Dodgers' Willie Crawford in defense of Ken Forsch. He was expected to return in a couple weeks but only played one more game in 1971, in late September.

the loss with five runs on eight hits, and sandwiched between flawless relief from Jim Ray and Denny Lemaster was Buddy Harris giving up the sixth run. The 6-1 loss was Houston's third in a row and their seventh in their last eight games. Two more games versus the Dodger Blue would follow when the calendar turned to the season's final month, but the Astros could only split the series if they won both.

No more talk around the Astros was about the pennant race, but rather increased discussion of a possible Jimmy Wynn deal during the offseason due to his lackluster season and his feud with skipper Walker.

Batting averages had risen throughout the team, with Bob Watson leading the team at .295, and followed by Jesus Alou's .286, Jack Hiatt's .276, Cesar Cedeno's .266, Denis Menke's .262, Joe Morgan's .261, Norm Miller's .260, rookie Rich Chiles' .245, and Doug Rader's .242. Even pitcher Ron Cook, who had taken Larry Dierker's spot in the rotation after he was placed on the disabled list, had marked up a .250 batting percentage. Jimmy Wynn was still underperforming at .214, and Roger Metzger, established by now mainly as a defensive asset, was only batting .240. The month ended with both a four-game and three-game losing streak that was prevented from being an eight-game

Aaron Pointer, former Houston outfield prospect, succeeded in Japan in 1971 and later became an NFL referee.

skid only by a win over the Pirates. Regardless, the homestand was already the worst one in Astros history, and the second worst in franchise history behind a 3-10 stretch in 1962 when the team was still named the Colt .45s.[23] August was the worst month of 1971 for Houston, going 11-18, a .379 winning percentage (Or maybe "losing percentage" would be more fitting). In addition to the injuries that already were plaguing the Orange Crush, Doug Rader left Tuesday's game in the sixth inning to nurse an ailing shoulder. Former Astro Aaron Pointer, now playing in Japan, led the Nishitetsu Lions to a 13-1 win with a three-run home run, a spark the Astros surely wish they could have right about now.[24]

SEPTEMBER

BETTER LATE THAN NEVER?

I t was now the last month of the 1971 season. Any preseason prophecies about the Astros making a run for the pennant would have to be fulfilled by a miracle run to catch up to the San Francisco Giants. That would first include taking over the Los Angeles Dodgers, who entered September with back-to-back wins under the Astrodome, and began the month with another one. By a lopsided tally of 9-2, an eight-run second inning forced Astros starting pitcher Jack Billingham and long reliever Denny Lemaster out before Buddy Harris could finally put out the fire. Willie Davis began the onslaught with a single to score Maury Wills in the first inning, who ignited the disastrous second frame. He hit a ground ball that should have been an inning-ending double play, but after Joe Morgan stepped on second base to putout pitcher Don Sutton, his throw to first was off, allowing for Jim Lefebvre and Tom Haller to touch home for the Dodgers' second and third runs. From there, five straight singles extended the inning to a 41-minute half-frame and raised the LA tally from three to nine.

The only answer the Spacemen had came in the fifth inning. Johnny Edwards hit Sutton hard with a leadoff double, and Cesar Geronimo hit a triple, scoring Edwards. Two batters later, Joe Morgan brought Geronimo home on a fielder's choice groundout that retired Marty Martinez at second. Morgan was left stranded on first, and that is how the rest of the Astros night went. It was their fourth loss in a row and their eighth loss in nine games. Luckily, the tide was about to change.

September in baseball means roster expansion, and the Astros called up nine players from Oklahoma City, including John Mayberry and Ray Busse again and Derrel Thomas for his first time being added to a big league roster. In addition to the three position players, six pitchers moved their lockers from All Sports Stadium in OKC to the Astrodome in Houston, as Tom Griffin, Scipio Spinks, and Bill Greif were coming back, Skip Guinn was coming back to the big league squad for the first time in 1971 after short stints in Houston the prior two seasons, and Larry Yount and James Rodney Richard were getting their first taste of MLB.[1]

Tom Griffin lit up the big leagues in his rookie season in 1969 by striking out over 200 batters and leading the National League in strikeouts per nine innings, but for unknown reasons, he was only given the chance to pitch in ten games in 1971, going 0-and-6.

The temperamental Don Wilson was scheduled to pitch on September 2 to wrap up the horrendous Domestand. He gave his overworked bullpen a rest by going all nine innings, giving up three runs, two earned. However, none of those runs would matter once the game was through. Bob Watson helped the Astros score first with a base hit to left field, scoring Jesus Alou and Cesar Cedeno. Four innings later, with the Dodgers now ahead 3-2, Marty Martinez, Wilson, and Joe Morgan loaded the bases when Cedeno stepped up. He hit a Claude Osteen pitch just well enough to bloop it into shallow right field. Second baseman Jim Lefebvre and right fielder Bill Buckner went after it, but they collided with each other and neither came up with the ball, which was rolling away toward the right field corner, where it settled on the warning track.[2] The speedy Orange Crush, including Cedeno, looked like the Orange Flash as they rounded the bases for a rare inside-the-park grand slam to put the Astros back in front, 6-3. The 170-foot home run was the shortest such hit in the Astrodome in 1971, and a kind of hit that neither team's manager, Dodger's Walter Alston in his 37 years in baseball nor the Astros' Harry Walker in his 35 years in the game, had ever seen before this day.[3]

Three insurance runs came in the eighth with only one hit, a double off the bat of Larry Howard. The Astros turned the tables and won with nine runs after a night when they allowed nine. If there was any doubt that Cedeno was back after a slow start to the season, his three-for-four night with three runs scored and four RBI proved that he was most certainly was. An exciting game and a much-needed win made the flight to San Francisco an easy one. For the first time, the Astros at home were vulnerable, and they hoped getting away would relieve the gloom and doom, when typically, it was the other way around given the unique playing circumstances of the roof, artificial turf, and air conditioning that they were used to, and other teams were not.

After a cold first two months of 1971, Cesar Cedeno showcased his elite skills once again to become the most dangerous part of the Astros' lineup and spark comparisons to Willie Mays.

Speaking of flights, a disadvantage that the Astros had that most other teams did not was their travel arrangements. The Dodgers were the only ballclub with a private plane, and other teams chartered planes to fly with efficiency and luxury. The Astros, however, flew commercially often, which included sitting and waiting in the terminal. This was on par with the plethora of actions taken by the organization that sometimes made the Astros players feel less than big league.[4]

To welcome the Astros on September 3, all the division-leading Giants did was give their opposition déjà vu by scoring sixteen runs, deeming the

Astros' six useless. Both Bob Watson and John Mayberry hit home runs, with Watson hitting two, which combined to give Houston five runs. Those were outmatched by long balls from Tito Fuentes, Bobby Bonds, and Dick Dietz. Willie Mays added three extra-base hits with a triple and two doubles. The bullpen got their workouts in after Wade Blasingame was knocked around for four runs, Jim Ray for three, George Culver for two, Buddy Harris for six, and Denny Lemaster for one. Ray lost his fourth game, although Juan Marichal did not pitch five innings as the Orange Crush got their six runs on seven hits off the Dominican Dandy. Jim Barr relieved him in the fifth and pitched one pitch, which Johnny Edwards popped out on, and his lineup gave him the lead in the bottom half of the inning. Barr was relieved the next frame, so he only threw one pitch, yet still earned his first big league win.

A true pitcher's duel was on tap the next day. Ken Forsch and Don Carrithers combined to allow only one run on five hits. A solo home run from Bobby Bonds was the only loud contact of the day. A Sunday doubleheader on September 5 began with an encore of that in the Astros' favor; a 1-0 score and just eleven hits from both teams combined, with Jack Billingham striking out eleven in his work against Gaylord Perry. In the first inning, the Giants were dealt a blow when Willie McCovey was hit in his throwing hand with a sharp Joe Morgan ground ball, and it tore the skin between the thumb and index finger. Rookie Ray Busse, in just his fourth Major League game, reached first base when his ground ball that could have resulted in a double play was fielded by Perry, who made a throwing error past second and into center field that allowed Denis Menke to score from second base.[5] The Astros swept the doubleheader by putting up a 5-3 score in the second game, largely credited to both Cesars—Geronimo and Cedeno—racking up back-to-back RBI hits in both the third and fifth innings. In the fourth, Larry Howard singled in the remaining run to help beat Jim Willoughby, making his first appearance in the Majors. But the big story for Houston was the pitching.

The starting pitcher for the Astros was a man who, later in his career, would more than equal Larry Dierker's ace status for his teams, and some would say surpass Dierker's ability to establish himself as one of the greatest pitchers in Astros history. It all started in this second game of a doubleheader at Candlestick Park against the first-place Giants. James Rodney "J.R." Richard, measuring six feet and eight inches tall, also took the mound for his big league debut, and he gave his club a sneak peak of what he would give them in future seasons, and what he could have given them in the stretch run had the Astros been in it by this point. Richard, feeling "as natural as rain," pitched all nine innings, a complete game victory, and along the way, he struck out fifteen Giants, including Willie Mays three times and Bobby Bonds twice.[6] Mays said after the game that he would never again play when Richard was pitching against his team.[7]

September 1971 saw the big league debut of 6'8" J.R. Richard, who began his career by striking out fifteen Giants and winning one more game in the month. Even in his first loss, he still struck out nine Braves.

The Astros departed from cool, windy San Francisco to hot, humid Atlanta for two games and, as it turned out, two more wins. Scipio Spinks, another young pitcher who was called up for September, made his first appearance in 1971 on September 6 and earned his first win at the big league level. Fittingly, his name "Scipio" is believed to mean "first" in Latin.[8] The Orange Crush scored six runs in two innings–the second and third–thanks in part to a Ray Busse RBI double in each frame and even a Spinks RBI single in the second. Earl Williams was the only Brave who could get ahold of Spinks, and the four Atlanta runs came from a single and home run from him.

The Astros were heating up, but the conversations about what could happen in the offseason were still being had. Mike Ramsey of *The Orange*

Leader reported a rumor that Dodger third base coach Danny Ozark could replace Harry Walker as the Astros' manager in 1972.[9] The dissention against Walker was leaking out into public knowledge through media, and it was revealed that the only time Walker really put effort into talking with players was in Spring Training.[10] Past that, bench players were lucky to get anything more than a notification that they were pinch-hitting, but not by name–by a point of a finger and an informal command to get a bat.[11]

Scipio Spinks, who had one of the most unique names in baseball, earned his first Major League win in September 1971 after also earning September call-ups the prior two seasons.

Don Wilson put on a show for the Atlanta crowd, much to their chagrin, by allowing one run on two hits in a complete game. The Braves' Ron Reed was touched for four runs on eight hits and was pulled in the fourth after a dangerous orange attack that included back-to-back home runs from the unlikely Cesar Geronimo and the more likely Joe Morgan. Geronimo's was his first Major League home run, and it also brought home Wilson. Three batters later, Doug Rader plated Cesar Cedeno with a double, and that was the end of the road for Reed. Ray Busse singled home another run in the eighth to sweeten the win just a little bit more.

Two days off kept the Orange Crush flowing into Cincinnati, where on September 10 in the first game of a three-game series, the Cesars' effort of Geronimo reaching base on a fielder's choice and Cedeno doubling him home was enough to back up Jack Billingham's two-hit shutout against his and Geronimo's future team. More stellar Houston pitching came the next day with J.R. Richard getting the ball again. Despite surrendering his first home run off the first batter he faced in Pete Rose, Richard powered through a middle finger blister to allow only one other hit in five innings to get the win.[12] George Culver was credited with a hold and Fred Gladding with a save. Plus, John Mayberry countered Rose's blast with one of his own, his coming with Doug Rader on base to put Houston in front. Joe Morgan and Cedeno brought in two more runs in the eighth, and Mayberry launched a solo shot in the ninth to add to what became a 5-2 final.

Both Mayberry and Cedeno went deep on Sunday, September 12, to pace now-ace Don Wilson's two-run complete game. Mayberry's recent success was attributed to him losing some weight, going from 230lbs and 18 years old to now 217lbs at 21 years old to refine his six-foot, four-inch frame. The Astros, now in fourth place after winning seven in a row and sweeping two consecutive series, headed back to Houston, hoping that the Eighth Wonder of the World would once again become Dome Sweet Dome when they faced the San Diego Padres.

John Mayberry took advantage of September when he played more than any other month in 1971 to showcase his reliable, up-and-coming stardom with five home runs. If only the Astros could keep him…

Unfortunately, before the next game even started in the Astrodome, third baseman Doug Rader was admitted into Methodist Hospital in Houston in preparation for left shoulder surgery. He said the shoulder had been bothering him most of the season, particularly after dislocating it, and he even had to leave the game on September 1 early due to the discomfort.[13] He first dislocated his shoulder when he fell trying to field a ground ball in May in Philadelphia.[14] He tweaked the shoulder again on a similar play on July 9 in St. Louis.[15] The injured shoulder may be to blame for his drop-off after a career-year at that point in 1970.[16] He dropped from a .252 batting average and 25 home runs in 1970 to .244 and 12 home runs in 1971. Denis Menke took over third base duties for most of the remainder of the season, since all the Astros needed was someone to fill the spot for two and a half more weeks.

A shoulder dislocation in May was tweaked again in July and necessitated surgery in September, putting the "Red Rooster" out of the lineup and moving Denis Menke to the hot corner for the last two weeks of the season.

September 13 went the Astros' way. The Padres were headed for the win column as Clay Kirby had a no-hitter going through seven and San Diego left fielder Leron Lee jumped and snagged a Cesar Cedeno line drive to take away an extra-base hit in the fourth inning. In the eighth, Johnny Edwards hit a double to break up the no-hitter, then Roger Metzger and Joe Morgan hit a single and a triple to tie the game at two. In the bottom of the ninth with two outs, Cesar Geronimo reached first base on an error by first sacker Nate Colbert, who dropped a pop fly. Geronimo promptly stole second, and Denis Menke got on with another error, this time by third baseman Garry Jestadt on a ground ball, and Geronimo did his thing and sped around third to walk it off. Despite being outhit 9-3, the Astros won the game 3-2, a one-run triumph.

A wild first inning from Wade Blasingame contributed to a five-run first inning in the second game of the short series, and former Astro signee

Ed Acosta and the Padres rode that until the end to win 5-2 and snap the Astros' eight-game winning streak. The string of wins was the longest they would have in 1971. The Braves visited next, and on the same day Doug Rader went under the knife, Phil Niekro started and finished on September 15 while giving up two runs on four hits, one of the runs being unearned. Hank Aaron touched Jack Billingham in the fifth inning for a home run, his 44th of the season.

In the ninth inning, prospect Larry Yount was called on to pitch and make his Major League debut. He had not thrown last in a week due to military duty, but he was not going to pass up his opportunity to make his debut.[17] During his warmup throws on the mound, his arm tightened up, and he could not throw a single regulation pitch, so Jim Ray replaced him. Yount never got another chance to play in a Major League game, making him the only pitcher in MLB history to appear in a game yet be credited with zero batters faced. His younger brother Robin, on the other hand, later had a Hall of Fame career as a shortstop.

Pitching prospect Larry Yount made the shortest appearance of any Astro in 1971 – or any player ever for that matter – when he took to the mound to warm up in relief but had to leave before throwing an official pitch due to arm trouble. That opportunity would not find him again.

Pat Jarvis continued his dominance over the Astros on September 16, and he pitched four innings of one-hit relief of Tom Kelley to earn the win over J.R. Richard, who was saddled with his first loss after giving up four runs in seven innings.

The Reds replaced the Braves in the visitors' clubhouse for the weekend. September 17 saw another exciting Houston win as Don Wilson pitched a complete-game one-hitter and brought in two runs with two RBI singles, one of them a suicide squeeze, and the infield completed their second triple play of the season and of the history of the franchise. The bases were loaded this time as well, and Joe Morgan dove for and caught a line drive off the bat of Darrell Chaney. Morgan tossed to Roger Metzger to putout George Foster from second base, then Metzger threw to John Mayberry at first to retire Pat Corrales and the side.[18]

September 18, the last day game the Astros played in 1971, was lost on a heartbreaker as Woody Woodward scored on a George Culver wild pitch in the eleventh inning, and the Astros had no answer in the bottom half. The Astros celebrated Joe Morgan's birthday on September 19 by also going eleven innings, but this time winning with five unanswered runs, capitalized by Morgan's walk-off home run. The game-ending blast was Morgan's thirteenth of the season, which led the team. He expressed concern about him leading the Astros in homers back in May, saying that his club would finish in fifth place if that were to happen. Doug Rader had twelve when he had his procedure done, and Cesar Cedeno, who went 4-for-4 in this game, had ten. No one else had double-digits in long balls.[19] The lack of power, much in part due to the off-year of Jimmy Wynn, was one reason why the Astros did not stay in the pennant race consistently over the course of the season and were officially eliminated from contention on this day when the Giants also won.

Joe Morgan in 1971 led both the Astros and league in triples as well as the ballcub in home runs, the latter being a circumstance he hoped he would not reach since he felt that would indicate a lack of power from everyone else on the team.

After an off day, the Giants were the last visiting team to grace the AstroTurf in 1971 as the final homestand and Fan Appreciation Week wrapped up. Jack Billingham went the distance giving up one run on five hits, the run coming off a Willie McCovey homer, but a Cesar Cedeno double to bring home Joe Morgan and a Larry Howard solo home run sealed the deal for the last Astros win at home in 1971. The Giants took the last two, reversing the 3-1 score in their favor the second game in Juan Marichal's complete game. It was a short start for J.R. Richard, who only gave up one run on one hit but walked the first two batters he faced, then an RBI single by Bobby Bonds, followed by another walk which prompted Harry Walker to bring in George Culver. After Culver's three innings, Tom Griffin came in for two, during the second of which he surrendered a solo shot to Bonds to give the Giants a lead they would keep. The last home game in the Astrodome of the 1971 season was also a loss, and as in typical 1971 Astros fashion, it was by a single run, 2-1. Willie McCovey and John Mayberry both put balls into the bleachers, but McCovey was later hit by a Don Wilson pitch with the bases loaded to bring in the winning run in the fifth inning. Based upon how Harry Walker was using his bullpen, Marichal accused Walker of trying to keep San Francisco from winning the division against the Dodgers.[20] A fan had a sign up in the Astrodome that said, "FAREWELL HARRY, YOU'RE OLD 'HAT.'"[21]

Late Tuesday night, a vote by American League owners allowed for the Washington Senators to relocate. Three years after the Dallas-Fort Worth area was denied an expansion team and Judge Roy Hofheinz was blamed for trying to keep the Texas market all for himself, the Senators would move to Arlington. Ted Williams accompanied the team to continue managing them, though Mickey Mantle expressed interest in taking the reins.[22] Spec Richardson welcomed the move and did not believe that it would infringe upon Houston's market and fan base.[23]

There were two more series left to play, both in Southern California, with the first being in San Diego. A doubleheader was required because the football San Diego Chargers game took priority, so that day's contest would be played as part of a nighttime doubleheader on Friday. The regularly scheduled game was played first, and it lasted twenty-one innings for five hours and twenty-five minutes, the longest game in the National League in 1971. Ken Forsch only gave up one run in thirteen innings, and the bullpen allowed an additional seven hits over the next eight innings.

After pitching three innings in game one of a late-September doubleheader in San Diego, which lasted 21 innings, George Culver used two fog delays in game 2 to relax with booze in game two. Luckily, he and Jim Ray were not caught, nor did either pitch that game.

Clay Kirby pitched fifteen innings and only surrendered a single tally as well, off Rich Chiles' second home run of the season, but in the top of the twenty-first inning, with Denis Menke at bat, Padres pitcher Gary Ross, in his third inning of work, balked, allowing Jesus Alou to score, making the score 2-1. Bill Greif and Skip Guinn worked around two singles to win it for the Astros and mercifully end the marathon… so that both teams could prepare for the second game of the doubleheader!

The second game was more routine, lasting just two hours and fifteen minutes. After having to be woken up from sleep since the first game lasted so long, Scipio Spinks started and allowed four runs in five and two-thirds innings.[24] Fred Gladding took the decision, a loss, after Ollie Brown's fly-ball was not easily seen by Jimmy Wynn in right field, even after the umpires paused the game twice earlier in the game, once around the fifth inning and again earlier in the ninth inning, to allow the fog to clear. Houston ballplayers, including George Culver, speculated that the game would be suspended during the first fog delay, but it was not, and once the fog cleared, the game resumed. The speculation became confidence when fog rolled in the second time, with Culver and Jim Ray feeling so sure the game would not be finished on this night that they took some beers out of a coaches' office. When the game was called upon to resume, those players were shocked, but they just packed some of the beers in the bullpen baseball bag to take with them.[25]

The ball dropped in for a hit, Don Mason scored, and the Padres took the second game.[26] The first game began at 6:04 p.m. Eastern Daylight Time in San Diego (9:04 p.m. EDT), and the second game ended at 2:28 a.m. (5:28 a.m. EDT) the next morning.[27] So technically, the doubleheader was played on September 25 rather than the 24th. It is unclear if Wynn simply missed sight of the last fly ball or if he let it drop intentionally, but pitcher Fred Gladding was mad because he could see the fly ball from the mound, and Wynn said to Spinks after the game "I could've caught that, but we'd have been here til five o' clock in the morning!"[28]

Later that day, Jack Billingham got all the help he needed in the very first frame. Four runs, courtesy of a two RBI double from Jimmy Wynn between two RBI singles from Cesar Cedeno and Larry Howard, did the job for the Orange Crush, and another run from a Marty Martinez single in the ninth tacked on another run just in case. Larry Stahl crushed a homer to give San Diego fans one thing to cheer about in this rubber match that the Astros won.

Before the Astros began their final series of the season in Los Angeles, two days off gave Judge Hofheinz time to bring to Houston manager Harry Walker and announce, in a noon press conference in his wheelchair, that Walker would indeed be rehired, along with the entire coaching staff and general manager Spec Richardson, for the 1972 season.[29] Both men most responsible for destroying the potential of the Orange Crush Astros were now being retained for even longer. However, Walker, despite his lack of a postseason berth so far in his tenure with the talent he had, was optimistic about 1972, specifically about Jimmy Wynn being able to rebound just as Walker himself did in his career after a .237 season that he made up for with a following .363 campaign.[30]

The news about Walker being re-signed certainly did not please the Astros' clubhouse, but they only had three more games to deal with him before the players could go home. However, for the opposing Dodgers, they were one game back for the NL West division crown. The Giants, whom they were competing against, arrived in San Diego after the Astros left. In Los Angeles, September 28 was a 2-1 loss for the Astros despite a complete-game by Don Wilson. The game was well pitched by both Wilson and Bill Singer, but someone had to lose it, and Bob Watson's fourth-inning RBI base hit was not quite enough to shield a Duke Sims home run and Maury Wills single, so the Astros were that someone.

Jimmy Wynn's "Stormy Monday" of his 1971 season had come to a close, and by that point, his attention shifted from the field to wondering if he would be traded or if Harry Walker would be fired.

The next night was the last showing of the Orange Crush, who put up crooked numbers in four innings and an additional run in another inning, adding up to eleven runs. The effort was highlighted in the fourth inning when Bob Watson connected solidly off Doyle Alexander and drove a ball deep over center field for a two-run home run, his ninth of the season. The win was sweetened when starter Ken Forsch shut out the Dodgers, and he even collected two singles.

Fortunately for the Dodgers, the Giants lost to the Padres on this night, so they were still in the race.

September 30, the last day of the season. The Astros were simply playing out their schedule after a promising season that did not live up to its potential, while the Dodgers were hanging on by the thinnest of margins for the division pennant. This game was changed from blacked out locally to televised locally so more Los Angeles fans could watch and see what their team did. Jack Billingham was the starting pitcher for Houston, while Don Sutton was entrusted with the ball for the Dodgers as they had to win for any chance of extending their season. The Giants were still up by one game, so if the Dodgers won and the Giants lost, there would be a tie. Any other outcome would result in the Giants advancing.

Both pitchers finished what they started on this day, and both gave up six hits and one run. But Sutton gave up *only* one run, while Billingham surrendered two, which made the difference for the Blue Crew to take the game and do what they needed to do. It made no difference though as the Giants also won to clinch the division and set up a clash with the Pirates in the National League Championship Series.

As for the Houston Astros, they were now finished, and looked to 1972 as perhaps their year, in classic "maybe next year" fashion.

OCTOBER
THE POSTSEASON AND THE ASTROS

Both best-of-five League Championship Series were set. In the National League, the Western Division winning San Francisco Giants hosted the first two games at Candlestick Park, then the Pittsburgh Pirates, who won the East despite Harry Walker believing the Cubs would win since they were more balanced, would host the next three at Three Rivers Stadium, if all three were necessary.[1] The Giants won Game 1 on October 2, but the Pirates took the next three to win the National League pennant at home.

The American League pennant series began on October 3 at Memorial Stadium, where the Eastern Division winning Baltimore Orioles welcomed the Western Division winning Oakland A's for two. The Orioles took both, as well as the next game at the Oakland Coliseum, to sweep the series and take the American League pennant, for the third time in a row.

The 1971 World Series pitted the Pirates against the Orioles, with games 1, 2, 6, and 7 played in Baltimore and games 3, 4, and 5 in Pittsburgh. The Pirates won Game 7 to win the World Series for the first time since 1960.

As for the Astros, they finished the season tied with the Reds for fourth place with a record of 79-83, the same record as 1970, but eleven games behind the Giants for first place. This was the final consecutive season that future Hall of Fame second baseman Joe Morgan would spend in Houston, and he made it a good one, compiling a .256 batting average, hitting

13 home runs, stealing 40 bases, and partnering with Roger Metzger for the National League triples lead with 11. They both also displayed sound defense. The Astros' most consistent hitters in 1971 were Morgan and Bob Watson, the latter of whom finished the campaign with a .288 batting average, 9 home runs, and 67 RBI. Cesar Cedeno, the only Astro with more runs batted in that Watson, was called up in June of 1970, so 1971 was his first full season at the big league level, and it did not take him long to adjust to indoor baseball on artificial turf as he led the National League with 40 doubles and led the club with 161 hits. 161 is also how many games Cedeno played in during the 1971 season, which ended up being his career-high, meaning he averaged a hit per game. In doing so, he set a franchise record at the time with 611 at-bats in a season. The one game he did not appear in was in the Dome against the Phillies on April 26, a one-run loss by a 2-1 score. The "Toy Cannon" Jimmy Wynn suffered the emotional effects of his offseason stab wound and divorce, causing him to have the worst season of his career, batting .203 with 7 home runs and even being booed and ridiculed by Houston fans later in the season.[2] Doug Rader participated in 28 double plays, only one shy of the league-leader Ron Santo, and won his second consecutive Gold Glove award at third base after becoming the first Houston player to win the award in 1970. Johnny Edwards was also fantastic defensively, leading National League catchers in fielding percentage for the third consecutive season.

On the mound, Larry Dierker began the season on pace to overshadow his 1969 All Star campaign by starting out 10-1 with a 1.59 ERA through the first week of June. Leading up to the All Star Game, there were discussions of Dierker starting the game for the National League until his arm began to hurt too much.[3] Don Wilson took his spot as he was amid a career season himself, finishing 1971 with a 2.45 ERA and 16 wins, earning Astros MVP for 1971. An interesting batting story for Houston was that Wilson's seven RBI on the season was second on the ballclub among pitchers, behind Wade Blasingame's nine. Ken Forsch made a mark in his first full big league season, piling up an even 8-8 record and a 2.53 ERA. The bullpen was a strong point for the Astros in 1971, contrary to past seasons. Closer Fred Gladding finished with an ERA of 2.10, and his setup man Jim Ray was not far behind at 2.12. George Culver's 2.64 ERA made 1971 his best season in an Astro uniform.

The team played a game better on the road than at home, going 40-41 away from Houston and 39-42 under the Astrodome, the latter being thirteen games under the 58-29 home record the team was on pace for to begin the season. This was contrary to how the Astros performed in seasons past, as the Dome's unique atmosphere typically gave them a home-field advantage. The Dome's advantage led to the Astros finishing last in all of baseball in home runs (Though the pitching staff led all of baseball by surrendering the least number of homers) but third in triples in both the National League and all of baseball, as well as second in baseball in doubles, leading the NL in two-baggers. When facing the eventual division-winning Giants, each club split 18 games, giving both teams a 9-9 record against one another. The Astros won the season series against the Cubs, Reds, Phillies, and Padres, and split the season matchups versus the Braves and Giants. They struggled the most against the Expos, Pirates, and Cardinals, with a 4-8 record against the first two and a 2-10 split versus the Redbirds.

The 1971 Astros set an MLB record by playing in 75 one-run games, of which they won 32 and lost 43. Had they played those games with the opposite record of 43-32, they would have tied with the Giants for first place, assuming any of those newly found wins were not against them, in which case the Astros take the division crown.[4]

Baseball statistician Bill James once discovered a relationship between the amount of runs a team scores and allows, and the amount of wins they *should* have accumulated based upon those numbers when they are used in a specific formula. The concept is known as the Pythagorean Win Loss due to its similarity to the Pythagorean Theorem. The formula is written as so:

$$\frac{\text{Runs scored}^2}{\text{Runs scored}^2 + \text{Runs allowed}^2}$$

Some sources use 1.8 or 1.83 as a more accurate power in the equation.[5]

While achieving a record of 79-83, the 1971 Astros scored 585 runs and allowed 567. Using those two numbers and inserting them where appropriate into the equation, Pythagorean Win Loss shows that the Astros should have put together the exact opposite record, 83-79, a four-game improvement. That would have made 1971 the first winning season in franchise history, not counting if any of the poor executive decisions leading up to 1971 had not been made. The team would have finished in third place, where they stood for most of June and July.

With so many statistics against the Astros for 1971, it can be difficult for some to imagine that this team should have won the pennant looking back. However, after considering what the organization and the roster of the team would have looked like had some negative doings simply not been done in the seasons from 1965 until this point, the possibility of the Orange Crush bringing an elite winner to Houston in 1971 becomes far clearer, perhaps even making some players and fans from that era groan when they realize how close their team was to turning oranges into orange juice.

WHAT COULD HAVE BEEN

WHAT COULD HAVE BEEN:
THE TEAM

With the help of money from co-owner R.E. Bob Smith, the vision of an aggressive small-ball team from general manager Paul Richards, and the scouting genius of the scouting team under farm system director Tal Smith, the Houston Major League ballclub signed more eventual big leaguers from 1961 to 1973 than any other team did.[1] Since most of that work was spoiled by later general manager Spec Richardson, we can revisit those poor decisions and get a glimpse of what the Astros could have looked like had someone else been given the role other than Spec Richardson.

When it comes to the roster moves, good and bad, that were made or could have/should have been made or not been made, those stem from the general manager. As for who it should have been, Spec Richardson can be ruled out easily due to his inexperience in the role at the time that later drained the club of its reserve of young talent. Paul Richards, nicknamed the "Waxahachie Wizard" due to his origin from Waxahachie, Texas, held the title when many of those key players were signed during the Colt 45s days and the earliest days of the Astros, and he was often considered a genius for this reason. However, in the days before the Major League Baseball Draft, which was introduced in 1965, a team's general manager was not always as involved in signing and developing young players as they are today; rather the organization's scouting and farm system specialized in that, though Richards did like having control and so he did involve himself some, such as when he took visits to watch some top prospects (Larry Dierker and Doug Rader among them, and he offered those players their contracts directly).[2] Knowing this and combining it with the fact that Richards was often criticized for being tough to get along with since he had a sly and cocky demeanor, and wanted much credit (A common desire among some early Astros executives), this makes his firing in 1965 by Judge Hofheinz more understandable. Richards' final words when he was dismissed say it all: *Houston Post* writer Mickey Herskowitz tried to console Richards by saying that "the Judge is his own worst enemy," to which the Waxahachie Wizard replied, "Not while I'm alive he isn't."[3]

In 1966, the trio of Spec Richardson, Tal Smith, and new field manager Grady Hatton took over the general manager role, though they did not use that phrase. Of the three, Richardson was more acclimated to business and finance, and of course the team's skipper needs to be free to

Tal Smith wore several hats for the Houston Major League franchise in its early years, being involved in the team's scouting as well as the construction of the Astrodome, and he also held a portion of the team's general management duties in 1966.

put most of his focus on managing the club in the dugout. Smith had proven himself in several ways, beginning with presiding over the farm system and scouting department when they signed the likes of Rusty Staub, Joe Morgan, Sonny Jackson, Doug Rader, Bob Watson, Larry Dierker, Don Wilson, and plenty of others. At the same time, many of the players who were signed were done so due to Paul Richards having that vision of small ball for his ballclub.[4] However, it was Smith who was the primary liaison for ensuring that the Astrodome would be suitable for baseball to be played inside, which included finding what would become AstroTurf, and then, of course, he shared general management duties with Richardson and Hatton for a season. Meanwhile, he also added to his plate the role of vice president, director of player personnel.[5] Paul Richards was certainly a mastermind of the organizational structure both in the front office and on the field, so he is the easy first choice for appropriate general manager for the Astros. The argument can certainly be made for Tal Smith as well, as no one else had earned the chance to get the job of general manager and proven himself to be fit for it, more than Smith, and it was his ability to successfully conduct operations that is one reason why he was inducted into the Astros Hall of Fame in 2022.

The likely best-case scenario is this: If Richards is allowed to hang around for the long term, great. That means the organization gets the benefits of both Richards as GM and Tal Smith as farm system director and vice president, player personnel. However, if Richards still must get the boot, and a new GM needs to be chosen in 1967, that is okay too, because Smith is the obvious best choice to keep the farm system growing and the big league club's chances rising.

On the field, starting at the catcher position, the 1971 team had Johnny Edwards, Jack Hiatt, and Larry Howard. It was at this position where Richards made one of his only mistakes: he traded Jerry Grote to the Mets for pitcher Tom Parsons after the 1965 season. Grote was kept in Oklahoma City for all of 1965, leaving John Bateman and Ron Brand to do the catching in Houston, and both were

Catcher Jerry Grote never played for the Astros, but he began his career with the Colt 45s and became a star in New York with the Mets after being traded after the 1965 season.

left unprotected in the 1968 Expansion Draft once Edwards was acquired via trade. Grote was one of the top prospects signed by Richards in 1962, having been the starting catcher in the game during which the Colt 45s fielded an all-rookie starting lineup on September 27, 1963.[6] Once he got to New York, he became accustomed to playing a full Major League season and grew into one of the National League's best defensive catchers. Lou Brock said that Grote was the toughest catcher for him to steal bases off. Grote also added great rapport with pitchers and a good bat.

Jack Hiatt was a purchase from the Cubs before 1971, and while he provided some excellent hitting at points during the season, if the team has Grote and Edwards, Hiatt is not needed, and Larry Howard is kept in Oklahoma City. The reality of the Astros having both Jerry Grote and Johnny Edwards on the same roster is alluring, but is it very likely?

More so than you think. Since Grote was homegrown (and relatively local, as he was from San Antonio), Paul Richards, barring his mistake of giving up on the young backstop, would have wanted to keep his players around. Edwards was on the Cardinals in 1968, when he was traded to Houston, and since St. Louis had Tim McCarver already, the Cards were actively trying to shop Edwards. This is evident by the fact that the trade to send Edwards to Houston was already structured and in place before the 1968 World Series, which the Cardinals were in, even started. The deal simply could not be executed until after the Series. Even before he arrived in St. Louis in 1968, the Cincinnati Reds needed to part with him as Johnny Bench was coming up from the minor leagues, meaning that at the time the Astros acquired Edwards, he was not considered a front-line starting catcher like he became in Houston. Given the Cardinals' apparently strong desire and need to part with Edwards, and the fact that he would provide for Grote both a good veteran mentor who had played in the World Series in 1961 and a left-handed bat to platoon with and give days off, it is not unthinkable that a different general manager would have seen the acquisition of Edwards to join Grote as viable.

However, that is not the only potential dilemma from Edwards joining the Astros. In that October 11 trade, workhorse pitcher Dave Giusti was given to the Cardinals in return. Three days later, the Cards dealt him to the new San Diego Padres, who later traded him right back to St. Louis.

This was because Spec Richardson had heard that the Padres were interested in Giusti, so Richardson's logic was to trade Giusti and get something for him rather than just let him get plucked in the expansion draft.

Par for the course for Richardson, since using that logic, he could have simply protected Giusti the same way he protected Edwards, or, if Richardson had to deal Giusti away, he could have even traded Giusti to the Padres directly. Or, given that the Cardinals then lost Giusti to the expansion draft then put together a sufficient trade package to get Giusti back, why couldn't the Astros have done the same? Not only that, the Cardinals evidently were not keen on keeping him in the first place, since they were not only willing to take the risk of losing Giusti altogether by trading him to San Diego with the hopes of trading for him back, but also, a season-and-a-half later, the Cardinals dealt Giusti to the Pirates.[7]

Confused? Exactly. Why put any of the three ballclubs involved (Astros, Cardinals, Padres) through all this trouble?

Dave Giusti spent most of his tenure in Houston as a starting pitcher, but he got his break in Pittsburgh as a closer. One can imagine how well he would have done in that role in the pitcher-friendly Astrodome.

Because of this, and because the Cards were evidently anxious to deal away Edwards, that trade between the Cards and Astros could have been easily constructed differently by a smarter general manager so that Giusti, who was a homegrown prospect who joined the franchise in 1961 before the team even began play, remains in Houston. It was in 1971 after all that, in Pittsburgh, Giusti became the best closer in the league and helped the Pirates to the World Series Championship.

What would this reworked trade have looked like? We know that Edwards would go to Houston, and if St. Louis wanted to sweeten the deal at all, they could throw in outfielder Ron Davis, whom the Astros had previously and was a reliable hitter. In the spirit of giving players back, Hal Gilson could be sent from Houston to St. Louis, as well as two prospects of the Cardinals choosing, and cash thrown in if the Astros felt that they would be losing too much. That way, as we look back, we are not creating any huge butterfly effects that could drastically affect other teams.

From STL: Johnny Edwards, possibly Ron Davis

From HOU: Hal Gilson, two prospects, possibly $$$

That is a unique situation where we would want to avoid "double-dip-ping," but considering as many factors as possible, this trade, shedding the Cardinals of an aging catcher who was sitting behind McCarver for playing time and giving them some young players, is not hard to imagine happening in the fall of 1968.

Unfortunately, that is not the only time looking back at the late 60's and early 70's Astros that we see a case of "double-dipping" that would need rectification to make sense. Prospect-turned star right fielder Rusty Staub was deemed dispensable by the Astros for several reasons: He held out for more money, he sat out on the day of RFK's funeral against man-agement's wishes, he had an accidental racial run-in with Aaron Pointer in the clubhouse (Pointer will come back around when we get to the outfield), he did not get along with Harry Walker, and Richardson did not believe Staub had the legs to play for a long time.[8, 9] When Staub was foolishly sent to the Expos, the return was Jesus Alou, Skip Guinn, Jack Billingham, and $100,000. The latter two players and the money replaced Donn Clendenon, who refused to report to the Astros because he had no desire to play under Harry Walker again like he did in Pittsburgh. With someone different at the manager's helm, Clendenon likely reports, but the same front office that would have avoided Walker surely would not have traded Staub, making Clendenon a moot point in these discussions.

While Staub is an obvious keeper for the Astros given how well he developed and played during his years in Houston, as well as how well he did after leaving. Jack Billingham was a good, reliable arm, who Larry Dierker speculated "would have become one of the best setup men in the league."[10] He was primarily a starting pitcher, both in Houston and when he had his marquee years in Cincinnati, but he possessed a sinker/slider combination that induced a lot of ground balls for the defensively talented infield to turn into easy outs, which is great late in games.[11]

In the same way the trade for Johnny Edwards could have been easily negotiated differently by someone more knowledgeable than Spec Rich-

ardson before pulling the trigger, so could this one. The difference this time is that it was the Astros looking to part with someone rather than the other team, as Richardson did not like that Staub held out for more money before 1968 and that he sat out for the day of RFK's funeral, which was a point of contention for Richardson with Giusti as well. Staub also did not get along with Harry Walker, like several players in the clubhouse. So this time, the Astros initiated the trade, which could make the dialogue between the Astros and Expos leading up to a deal a little trickier, but once we look at the potential trade, that backstory will write itself.

Both Howie Reed and Leo Marentette were sold by the Astros to the Expos on April 3, 1969, five days

Jack Billingham spent most of the 1960's in the Dodgers' minor league system until the 1968 Expansion Draft sent him to Montreal before the Astros then traded for him. He had experience yet was young enough to become a dependable and talented arm in Houston.

before Billingham was sent to the Astros to complete the Staub deal. Since this means that the two clubs were in communication outside of the goings-on with the Staub deal, why not just get Billingham in exchange for those two guys? The Expos' focus before their inaugural season in 1969 was signing young prospects whom they could develop, and while Billingham had not played in the Majors for very long, he was originally signed into pro ball in 1961 and was 26 when the Expos sent him to Houston, making him perhaps just a bit older than what they wanted. Expansion teams typically have players who are veterans trying to hold on and young guys trying to catch on, and with Reed and Marentette, the Expos were getting one of each. This way, both teams are no worse off, there are no butterfly effects, and Billingham remains an Astro as he was in 1971.

From MON: Jack Billingham

From HOU: Leo Marentette, Howie Reed

Finally, Bob Watson was a catcher growing up, but injuries both in the minor leagues and at Wrigley Field hurt his shoulder, his ankles, and ended his catching days for good. The front office under Richardson was always looking for veterans, particularly first baseman, rather than letting the young guns develop. Had Watson been kept at the Major League level after his September 1966 callup, and had a different manager not done what Harry Walker did and put the Bull in the leadoff spot to start a game against the Cubs on a misty Chicago day on July 30, 1968, Watson likely does not break his ankle running the bases that day, and he develops sooner into a catcher, first baseman, and outfielder, though first base would be his primary position as Edwards and Grote would be behind the plate and there were faster outfielders on the team.[12]

Watson is the easy answer for first base for the Astros as he was a talented, homegrown hitter who adapted his swing to the Astrodome so that he would hit more line drives and bring in more runs. As John Mayberry matures and gets more experience, he becomes the number two guy, and possibly even a platoon partner because he batted left-handed and was a power threat. If Nate Colbert, an athletic first baseman who was selected by Houston from St. Louis in the 1965 Rule 5 draft and who came up with the Astros, had been protected in the 1968 Expansion Draft rather than being made available due to slow batting development and Harry Walker's dislike of Colbert's skin color, he would be the next man up waiting in Oklahoma City. If Colbert was able to keep his speed while developing his bat, then perhaps over time, he would have surpassed Watson as the righty-swinging first baseman with a shooting star on his chest.

Nate Colbert toggled between Oklahoma City and Houston as he developed into a stable big leaguer, but his opportunity to play everyday at the highest level did not come until he joined the expansion Padres in 1969.

Denis Menke was shifted to first base in 1971 after Roger Metzger won the starting shortstop job, which takes us to shortstop. Metzger was acquired from the Cubs for Hector Torres in 1970 to complete a deal that sent Joe Pepitone to Chicago. Pepitone came to Houston in exchange for Curt Blefary, and Blefary was the Orioles' consolation for Mike Cuellar. Cuellar is arguably the worst trade of all the ones Spec Richardson made during his time as Astros general manager. The trade after the 1971 season that sent Joe Morgan, Denis Menke, Jack Billingham and Cesar Geronimo to the Reds caught the most headlines, but the Astros still had players who could take their spots. Cuellar's departure left a hole in the rotation in 1969 that Tom Griffin performed well enough in, but Cuellar won the Cy Young Award in 1969. Point being, if Cuellar is not traded, there is no Metzger.

Interesting point when it comes to Cuellar and Staub: Both were brought up by a Dallas-area sportswriter as good trade targets he believed the Astros should chase in June 1971, along with Nate Colbert. Dave Giusti and Jerry Grote were also mentioned as former members of the Houston club who were making headlines elsewhere.[13]

As for Menke, his bat was good enough for the Astros, but his defense was not at the level of the young Rookie of the Year finalist that Richardson gave up for him. Sonny Jackson excelled in his rookie season of 1966, batting .292, stealing 49 bases, and finishing second in ROY voting to the Reds' Tommy Helms, which, like Joe Morgan's runner-up to the Dodgers' Jim Lefebvre in 1965, seemed to be the wrong decision according to the stat lines. In both cases, the Astros' middle infielders had overall better numbers. Regardless, even though he regressed in 1967 as pitchers adjusted to him, Jackson's potential was higher in the Astrodome than in Atlanta's stadium due to it being a spacious pitcher's park that rewarded footspeed and defense. Defense in the Dome and on AstroTurf could be a tough thing to master, but those who did proved to be valuable for the team.

Even as other ballclubs installed AstroTurf in their ballparks, many of them omitted dirt infields and left dirt "pits" around the bases, which is easier to field on because there was no lip between slower dirt and quick AstroTurf. All these factors, plus the fact that a sophomore slump is no reason to trade someone, mean that the left-handed batting Jackson's best days were ahead of him in the Astro-

Sonny Jackson began his career as a Rookie of the Year runner-up but was traded to Atlanta after a "sophomore slump." His potential in the Astrodome never lived up to the expectations that a Sports Illustrated cover appearance indicated because of that.

dome as he continued to counter-adjust to pitchers and use the AstroTurf to his advantage to join Morgan in perhaps the best keystone sack combination in the National League. Maybe they even earn another showcase on the cover of Sports Illustrated.

Reversing the Jackson trade means that first baseman Chuck Harrison remains in Houston, and that Menke and Denny Lemaster remain in Atlanta. Lemaster was a decent starter and reliever, but the Houston pitching staff was getting deeper every season, so the vacancy would be filled quite easily by 1971.

The catcher, first base, and shortstop positions have been visited, as has second base with a brief mention of Joe Morgan, but there is another guy who Richardson got ahold of who would become an All Star second baseman. Sandy Alomar was a player-to-be-named-later in the trade that shipped Eddie Mathews from the Braves to the Astros, but in the same offseason, Alomar was sent to the Mets for Derrell Griffith. Alomar made his name in Anaheim, joining the American League All Star team in 1970, and he upped his batting average in 1971 from .251 to .260, as well as his home run total from two to four. Having Alomar behind Morgan

Few baseball fans think of Houston when Manny Mota comes up in conversation but had the Colt 45s kept him for the 1963 season and beyond, the same reliable and consistent hitting ability he became known for could have easily translated into similar success under the Dome.

would be the best insurance policy the Astros would have at any position other than catcher.

Another valuable player who was given up before even playing a game in Houston was outfielder Manny Mota. Mota, one of the greatest pinch-hitters of all time most known for his time with the Dodgers, was traded by the Giants to the Colt 45s in the offseason between 1962 and 1963 and was dealt to the Pirates in the same offseason. He regularly was a

.300 hitter both in the starting lineup and off the bench no matter where he played, whether it be in Pittsburgh, Montreal, or Los Angeles, and there is no reason to think that he could not have performed similarly under the Astrodome, where his hitting style would have worked very well.

Doug Rader had third base locked down with his spectacular defense and powerful bat, but in September, his left shoulder was bothering him enough to require surgery. He dislocated his shoulder in a game on May 9 in Philadelphia (The artificial turf was the newest in baseball as Veterans Stadium opened in 1971, so that might have made a difference) and tweaked it again exactly two months later on July 9 in the second game of a doubleheader, during which he hit a home run, in St. Louis. However, since the pitching staff for the Astros is now different, and therefore likely the lineups those pitchers face from opposing teams, a butterfly effect is created that could affect those ground balls:

Are they hit towards Rader? Are they hit slightly differently in a way that does not cause injury? Are they even hit on the ground, but rather line drives or fly balls? Are they even hit at all?

If we speculate this preventing his injury and remember Rader's still-solid stats as they were in 1971, perhaps this season becomes an encore of his career-year of 1970, which in turn becomes a turning point season in the Red Rooster's career. Those stats could have made the Red Rooster a candidate for the backup third baseman (Behind Joe Torre of the Cardinals) on the NL All Star squad, battling Ron Santo of the Cubs, who did make the squad, and Tony Perez of the Reds for that roster spot.

Even if Rader does somehow still become injured, he may have been able to postpone a shoulder surgery if it meant that he could play in the postseason, which would have been a more common decision in that day than today for big league ballplayers since they did not want to sit out and allow for someone else to get hot while filling in, and then the original player not play again, as the Wally Pipp story goes. Rader possibly could have put off surgery because he was still playing solidly in the week leading up to his operation, and if anything, he could have simply rested for most, if not all, of September to prepare for October. It would have only been an additional month that the surgery would have been put off since Rader had it in mid-September, and the World Series, if the Astros made it that far, would have ended in mid-October, so he could have went under the knife afterwards and been ready for Spring Training in February 1972, since he originally was reported to be ready in January, so adding another month would still have him ready to go to Cocoa Beach for the following season.

A fully healthy Doug Rader in 1971 might have delivered an encore to his standout 1970 season, the best of his career to that point.

This still, however, poses a necessary question: If Rader's injury still occurs and he either cannot or decides not to put off surgery until the offseason, who is the next man up at the hot corner? Denis Menke is staying in Atlanta since Sonny Jackson is still in Houston, so it is not him. The most likely candidate was also traded by Richardson to Atlanta. On December 4, 1968, the same day as the Cuellar trade, franchise fan-favorite and the last remaining player from the original 1962 Colt 45s roster Bob Aspromonte was shipped to Georgia for Marty Martinez. Aspromonte was another player whose bat was well-suited for the Dome, so if he stays in Houston until 1971, he would have had one more chance to play everyday in an Astros uniform and help the team in the postseason before he retired after the season.[14]

Now out of the infield and to the pasture. Rusty Staub is locked in right field, and he could play first base as well. Cesar Cedeno wanted to play right field in his first couple of seasons because he liked Roberto Clemente, until Jimmy Wynn motivated him by telling him that he is the face of the franchise and the one to become a star in center field.[15] Of course, with Staub sticking around, Cedeno's spot in center field is even more solidified by process of elimination, which also necessitates Wynn moving to left field. Cesar Geronimo's role in 1971 was often to substitute for another outfielder after their last at-bat, either in the field after they got out or on the basepaths if they reached base. That role would remain, and Geronimo filling in for Rusty Staub in late innings for speed and defense would become a regular sight on scorecards of Astros games. Righty Manny Mota and lefty Norm Miller, the "secret weapon," could also fill that role when Geronimo was starting or otherwise not available, or they could simply be additional reliable bats and outfielders.

Since the Orange Crush Astros were created using phenomenal farm system development, it is intriguing to consider the September call-up players and top minor league prospects. This relates to the outfield when discussing Aaron Pointer and Walt Williams, the former of whom was traded to the Cubs after a clubhouse feud with Rusty Staub.[16] Pointer had come up with the Colt 45s in 1963, including playing right field during the all-rookie lineup game on September 27, and he later got another taste of the majors in 1966 before winning the Astros' starting left field job going into the 1967 season. Eventually he faltered and Ron Davis took over, but Pointer was still considered a prospect for the outfield, as was Williams while he was with the Colt 45s in 1964 before being acquired by the Cardinals off waivers. Williams' hustling style of play at a diminutive size that helped him excel in Chicago with the White Sox could have easily added the same value in Houston both on the field and in the clubhouse.

The pitching staff is already set for the most part. It is a shame that the ace of the staff, Larry Dierker, had to miss the final two months of the regular season, because he was headed towards one of, if not the best, pitching season in Astros history. Had he been able to continue his pace of 10-1 with a 1.59 ERA throughout the season without arm trouble, he would have been projected to win at least 24 games (Meaning that Jim Owens' prediction of Dierker winning 25 games could have come to fruition) and he would still have the Astros' single-season records for wins and ERA, with Mike Hampton's 22 wins in 1999 and Nolan Ryan's 1.69 ERA in 1981 not being enough to supplant 1971 Dierker in those categories. Those two stats would have also led the NL in 1971, topping Tom Seaver's 1.76 ERA and that season's NL Cy Young Award winner Fergie Jenkins' 24 wins. Because of this potential, it is fun to imagine if Dierker could have kept pitching for the entire season and achieved those stats, as well as the NL All Star starting nod and the Cy Young Award, especially if the organization had not overused him early in his career as well as supplied a deeper pitching rotation around him and helped him develop more leg strength to take some of the load off his elbow.[17] In this scenario, he is about to get that.

Don Wilson follows him in the rotation. Mike Cuellar would be in the rotation, defying the organization's thought that he was too old.[18] It is probable that, if he replicated his dominance in Baltimore in Houston, with the help of the pitcher-friendly atmosphere, he could have been even better than he was in Baltimore, a scary thought for hitters. Perhaps he could have even surpassed Wilson to fill the number two spot in the rotation, or possibly even Dierker to become the ace. Ken Forsch and Tom Griffin, both having shown great potential, finish out a five-man rotation, if the manager elected to use five starters. This pitching rotation was so good that even with Dierker out for the last two months of the season, the Astros still had two starters in the top five in ERA in the National League, with Don Wilson and Ken Forsch finishing third and fourth, respectively. This means if Dierker had maintained

As phenomenal as starting pitcher Mike Cuellar was in Baltimore with the dynasty Orioles in the late 60's and early 70's, many proponents have voiced that he would have been even better in the Astrodome, a somehow likely outcome and a scary one for opposing batters.

his stellar ERA for the whole year, three of the top five ERA's in the NL would have belonged to Houston pitchers.

George Culver, Jim Ray and closer Fred Gladding already made the bullpen strong, and keeping Jack Billingham in the 'pen and realizing Dave Giusti's ability as a late-inning reliever in Houston only make it tougher for opposing batters late in ballgames, especially in the relatively dark Astrodome. Gladding and Giusti would battle it out in Cocoa for the closer job.

When discussing the bullpen, a likely scenario is that Mike Marshall remains with the Astros' organization. Marshall, who became the first relief

Mike Marshall jumped around from team to team early in his career because teams did not care for his unorthodox pitching philosophy, but his screwball was excellent, enough that would project success in the Dome.

pitcher to win the Cy Young award in 1974, was an Astro for a short time in early 1970, but was later dealt to Montreal for outfielder Don Bosch because management did not like him throwing a screwball.[19] Having more pitching, especially of Marshall's potential, is always beneficial for a ballclub that calls the Astrodome home. It is true that he was signed by Spec Richardson, but since the ballclub was always looking for young guys, especially pitchers, it is entirely reasonable to suspect that the organization would have still signed Marshall too. He then would have been available out of triple-A Oklahoma City.

A less likely possibility is the team keeping Joe Hoerner, the closer for the St. Louis Cardinals during their 1967 and 1968 pennant-winning seasons who was a Colt 45 for two seasons and made his big league debut during the all-rookie lineup game in September of 1963. The Cardinals selected him in the 1965 Rule 5 Draft, but managing to hang onto him would obviously add even more organizational depth to a pitching staff that is already stellar and to a bullpen that was one of the team's strengths in 1971. If Hoerner does stick around, this could result in the Astros not trading for Fred Gladding for the closer role, but with Hoerner's chronic health concerns, it is tough to say if it would have actually been much different with the Astros having Hoerner over Gladding. In all likelihood, if Hoerner remains in the Astros' organization, he is probably spending most of his time outside of Houston in the state just north of Texas at triple-A.

The author of the controversial *Ball Four*, Jim Bouton, covered the last month-and-a-half of the Astros' 1969 campaign, and he was demoted to triple-A and forced out of baseball in 1970 due to the backlash of his diary. However, this does not change his effectiveness in Houston, as the last thing a hitter wants to see is a knuckleball in the already-pitcher-friendly Astrodome. It is a stretch to say Bouton may have been able to stick it out and come back to the big leagues in 1971, but he did have a jersey made for him prior to Spring Training, so since we are considering what-if situations, we just never know.

The coaching staff in 1971 consisted of Buddy Hancken as bench coach, Jim Owens as pitching coach, Salty Parker as third base coach, and Hub Kittle as first base coach. Mel McGaha had been the manager of the triple-A club from 1966-1967 and the hitting and first base coach for the big league club since 1968, but he quit after 1970 to run the parks and recreation department in his hometown of Shreveport, Louisiana.[20] This left a spot open for Kittle, the manager at Oklahoma City in 1970, to be promoted to Houston. A team that appeared poised to contend for a World Series championship might have held off that decision for him for at least one more season and spread out the coaching duties to allow for more involvement, such as allowing Kittle to focus on pitchers in the bullpen since McGaha is coaching first base and hitters.

Since manager Harry Walker was not well-liked in the Astros clubhouse, to the extent that Pirates second baseman Bill Mazeroski warned

Joe Morgan of Walker becoming their team's skipper in 1968, there are two easy answers of who would have been a better option, both of whom being Walker's predecessors, Grady Hatton and Luman Harris.[21] Hatton had his credentials and good qualities, but as Walker easily proved, credentials don't necessarily make an ideal manager. The success his teams saw in Oklahoma City came with a different demeanor from Hatton, one that was endearing to players. Once he became the big league manager, he lost some of that and became temperamental, to the extent where he would manage from the runway tunnel if he was unhappy with the team's performance in a game.[22]

Hatton's predecessor, Luman Harris, was not only the first manager of the Astros (Not to be confused with the first manager of the franchise overall. The manager before him, Harry Craft, had been the manager while the ballclub still donned the Colt 45s name), but he was the opposite of both Walker and Hatton in personality. Joe Morgan described Harris as

"easygoing, tolerant, and very good baseball men from the old school. [He] knew what [he] wanted from [his] players, gave them room to do it, and then offered them full credit for whatever they accomplished." This obviously worked, as in 1969 as the manager of the Atlanta Braves, his team won the first NL West title. The only logistic in the way of Harris as skipper is that he was a Paul Richards yes-man, so when the former was terminated, so was the latter, which could still be the case in this scenario here. Morgan also recalled Harris not being much of a disciplinarian, while a young ballclub could

Mel McGaha has two stints managing in the Majors and was well-liked as a skipper in Houston's minor leagues, making him a viable candidate for manager of the Astros.

benefit from some discipline, if it is not too much, such as what Harry Walker provided.[23]

Three Astros coaches were well spoken of in research. Former triple-A Oklahoma City 89ers manager Hub Kittle was liked and respected by all the players, especially the pitchers who benefitted from his teachings and motivation. But alas, he was not interested in becoming a Major League manager.[24] Future Astros coach and skipper Bob Lillis was very well thought of during his playing days and his time as manager in Houston, and in 1971 he was a scout for the team, so he could also be considered, though at 40 years old entering the season, he might have been slightly too young to take the reins (Unless Hofheinz wanted to try to create the Sparky Anderson of the Astros, as he managed his first season with the Big Red Machine Cincinnati Reds in 1970 at age 35, becoming the youngest manager in baseball at that time). But another coach who also managed in OKC, before Kittle, was Mel McGaha. If a contending ballclub alone would not have been enough to keep McGaha from retiring, what about a promotion and a raise to manage said contending ballclub? He lived in Louisiana, which was and still is Astros territory, and it is where Rusty Staub was from, and he also had managed in the big leagues before, in Cleveland and Kansas City (A's). Add his local appeal to his big frame and easygoing yet matter-of-fact managing style, and Houston would have an ideal skipper. The team found success the last time the organization brought up a manager from Oklahoma City in Hatton, so why not try again with McGaha?

After all these considerations, had the Astros franchise retained a better general manager, which would have led to the retention and development under the Dome of all these fish that got away, mostly homegrown but some transplanted, they would have combined with the stable core that was kept around and formed an elite roster that looked something like this:

Lineup:[25]
SS Sonny Jackson 16
2B Joe Morgan 18
CF Cesar Cedeno 28
LF Jimmy Wynn 24
RF Rusty Staub 10
1B Bob Watson 27
3B Doug Rader 12
C Jerry Grote 8/Johnny Edwards 7

Rotation:
R Larry Dierker 49
R Don Wilson 40
L Mike Cuellar 35
R Ken Forsch 43
R Tom Griffin 38

Bullpen:
R George Culver 41*
R Jim Ray 45
R Jack Billingham 42
R Fred Gladding 48
R Dave Giusti 39 - Closer

Bench:
1B John Mayberry 33
2B Sandy Alomar 11
3B Bob Aspromonte 14
OF Manny Mota 15
CF Cesar Geronimo 20
RF Norm Miller 21

Coaching Staff:
Manager: Mel McGaha 1
Bench/Catching: Buddy Hancken 4
Pitching: Jim Owens 5
1B/Outfield/Bullpen: Hub Kittle 3
3B/Infield: Salty Parker 2

Minor League Prospects, September Call-Ups from Oklahoma City 89ers:
RHP Larry Yount 31
RHP Scipio Spinks 37
LHP Ron Cook 47*
RHP Bill Greif 44
RHP Buddy Harris 46
RHP J.R. Richard 50
LHP Joe Hoerner 52
RHP Mike Marshall 53
RHP Jim Bouton 56
C Larry Howard 13*
1B Nate Colbert 9*
1B Chuck Harrison 30*
2B Derrel Thomas 19
SS Ray Busse 25*
OF Jay Schlueter 17
OF Ron Davis 22
OF Aaron Pointer 23
OF Keith Lampard 26
OF Rich Chiles 29
OF Walt Williams 32*
…among others

(*Some of the uniform numbers have been improvised in cases that another player who was on the team first had a specific number before a player who had it later.)

As Mel Allen famously said, "How about that!"

Of course, now we must find the answer to the million-dollar question: How would this team have fared in 1971?

Using the Pythagorean Win Loss formula, we can take appropriate runs-scored and runs-allowed stats from each player and add them up appropriately to get a sense of what this team *should* have achieved. Starting with batters who were members of the 1971 Astros team already:

(*Note: For the sake of ease, with just two exceptions, players who were September call-ups or players who were given a "cup of coffee" will not be considered here*)

Joe Morgan: 87 scored
Cesar Cedeno: 85 scored
Bob Watson: 49 scored
John Mayberry: 16 scored
Cesar Geronimo: 13 scored

(*Another note: Pitchers will also be omitted from the runs scored total due to the happenstance nature of runs pitchers typically score*)

Since catcher Johnny Edwards would now be splitting time with Jerry Grote, we can simply half Edwards' runs scored total of 18 and use that 9 instead to get a fair number.

To compensate for Doug Rader's shoulder trouble, including the games he missed in late September, we can first take his 90 runs scored in 1970, his career year that he likely could have replicated if not for injury. Next, since he scored 51 in 135 games, if we translate that to 155 games, a good number of games we can suspect we would have played in, as well as how many games he played in 1969, that raises the run total to 53. But this still only gives us a number of runs scored if he had played the last two weeks of the season with his ailing shoulder. Since he is healthy in this scenario, we can take the average of 90 and 53, which is 71.5, and we will round down to 71 for realism and humility.

In the outfield, Norm Miller played so rarely because Harry Walker did not like him, so The Hat just decided to bench Miller out of the blue. While Miller would not have played as often as he did in 1969 when he played in over 100 games, he still would have played enough to make an impact. In 1970, Miller scored 29 runs in 90 games. That sounds fair.

Since Jimmy Wynn had a poor season that was in part due to off-the-field circumstances but also because of Harry Walker and the sustained uncertainty about the team and its ability to compete, perhaps if Wynn has an elite ballclub with better ownership and a better manager to come to Spring Training to, baseball becomes his escape and nirvana rather than part of his struggle. Since he was still dealing with issues outside of base-ball, at least an average season for Wynn follows, so take his 1968 season. He hit only 26 home runs rather than topping 30, and he also did not score 100 runs, but rather 85. That also sounds reasonable.

Johnny Edwards: 9 scored
Doug Rader: 71 scored
Norm Miller: 29 scored
Jimmy Wynn: 85 scored

Now let's add in the batters who had departed the Astros before 1971:

Rusty Staub: 94 scored
Bob Aspromonte: 21 scored
Manny Mota: 24 scored

As noted earlier, Jerry Grote's runs total will be divided by two. His total in 1971 was 35, an odd number that halves into 17.5, so once again, for the sake of believability, we will round it down to 17.

Jerry Grote: 17 scored

Some special consideration is needed with two middle infielders. We have already examined how Sonny Jackson's numbers would have been better in Houston because the playing atmosphere better suited his abilities. Because of this, we would be better using his runs scored total of 80 from 1966, when he showed his true potential. Sandy Alomar would have been used off the bench for the Astros, but in 1971 he was the Angels' starting second baseman. Therefore, it would fit his role better to use a number from a season in which that was his role. Take 1965 with the Braves, when he scored 16 runs in 67 games because Frank Bolling was the Braves' primary second baseman at the time.

Sonny Jackson: 80 scored
Sandy Alomar: 16 scored

To make the final addition of the numbers more dramatic, we'll save the runs scored total for later and go forward with the pitchers' runs allowed totals:

Larry Dierker: 50 allowed*
Don Wilson: 80 allowed
Ken Forsch: 60 allowed
George Culver: 33 allowed
Jim Ray: 27 allowed
Fred Gladding: 17 allowed
Scipio Spinks: 12 allowed**
J.R. Richard: 9 allowed**

(*Dierker's 50 runs allowed would remain the same whether he still gets hurt halfway through the season or whether he remains healthy. In the latter case, the runs he surrendered in games while he was plagued would simply be spread out over the rest of the season.)

(**Spinks and Richard are two exceptions to the September call-up rule stated earlier, because due to Spinks' previous cups of coffee with the

Astros and Richard's size and potential, they each could have possibly gotten their chances regardless of other circumstances, and possibly earlier in the season including making the club out of Spring Training.)

There are two discrepancies to cover in the rotation. Tom Griffin did not pitch much in 1971, for unknown reasons, but since his rookie season, like Sonny Jackson's, showed a lot of potential, using Griffin's rookie season of 1969 is a fair decision, and it would give him 80 runs allowed. Before the September callup of J.R. Richard, Griffin would likely have stayed in the starting rotation, so whether he gives up runs starting or out of the bullpen, it would probably even up to equal the same number of runs allowed over the course of the entire season.

As for the bullpen, Jack Billingham would have been a reliever on the Astros in this scenario, but he pitched exclusively as a starter in 1971. To get a reasonable number that Billingham could have achieved out of the bullpen, we will take his 1969 number of 45 runs allowed since he was a reliever that season (except for four games).

Tom Griffin: 80 allowed
Jack Billingham: 45 allowed
Now to add in the pitchers who left Houston before '71:
Dave Giusti: 31 allowed

Mike Cuellar surrendered 111 runs in 1971, but that was in Baltimore. Inside the pitcher-friendly Astrodome, we can imagine how much better he would have been, if that is even comprehensible. Therefore, his best in Houston, which came in 1966, is very possibly replicated, and he gave up 79 runs that year.

Mike Cuellar: 79 allowed

Now that we have all the numbers that we will need laid out, we need to add them up appropriately first before we can insert them into the Pythagorean Win Loss formula.

Total runs scored: 696
Total runs allowed: 523

Now to plug those numbers into the formula:

$$\frac{696^{1.83}}{696^{1.83} + 523^{1.83}}$$

The answer to that is a winning percentage of .627, which translates into a win/loss record of 102-60. However, since the 1971 Astros underperformed their Pythagorean win/loss record by four games, we can reasonably make the record four games "worse," still resulting in a projected win-loss record for the 1971 Houston Astros of **98-64**.

To some Astros fans, this may seem like a large, unrealistic number for the Astros of the late 60's and early 70's, but since we never got to see all these players together due to poor executive decisions and other circumstances, whether they be related or outstanding, there is no ground to refute this calculation! Besides, teams don't always play exactly as the Pythagorean Win/Loss record says they would have (Hence the four-game adjustment), and with the roster being composed differently and being under a different manager and general manager, some of the individual performances, and therefore the run totals from individual players, could have been slightly different based on how the team performed throughout the 1971 season and how Mel McGaha elected to utilize his players. For example, given that Cesar Cedeno hit .300 in his rookie season of 1970 and he broke out for his first elite season in 1972, perhaps he begins his breakout as one of the best center fielders in baseball a season earlier due to a different team dynamic around him, especially since his slump to begin the season may have been because of the lackluster clubhouse culture stemming from the poor trades, Harry Walker, and lack of postseason contention. The same could possibly apply to some of his teammates. Plus, runs scored do not indicate everything–a player can drive in a lot of runs and get on base a lot, but not score too many runs himself. Nevertheless, even if the Astros fall short of this exact record, they are still easily the NL West division champions.

Also, 1971 is the first season that the Astros had every position covered for all 162 games and were truly ready to become an elite team. To believe that this win/loss record would have been the team's result in 1971, it is also imperative to continue to consider the whole picture and evaluate how the prior seasons would have also played out differently. Imagine how exciting those years leading up to 1971 would have been as this team was developing! The team was still adapting to the Astrodome in 1965, and they experienced growth in 1966. Could 1967 have been the year the team finishes at .500 for the first time? Would they have finished in second place with a winning record in 1968, ready to pounce on the National League the next year? Would they have won the first NL West division title and the pennant in 1969? Would the 1970 Reds have won the division as easily as they did? In order to fully appreciate and understand how this 1971 team *could have, would have, and should have* come together, the entirety of the situation must be taken into account. That is why every aspect, from the attitudes of the ownership to the actions of general management, to the field manager, to the clubhouse demeanor and its causes, to the home-field advantage of the Astrodome, and of course the players that got away too soon, has been examined here.

Suddenly, teams like the Cardinals and Expos do not weigh the ballclub down so much, and the Giants and Dodgers are playing down to the wire at the end of the season… for a distant second place. Before then, the Astros send more representatives to the All Star Game than Larry Dierker, who did not play due to injury but otherwise might have started the game, and Don Wilson. Rusty Staub and Mike Cuellar made their fifth and third All Star teams in 1971, respectively, although if this remained the case in this scenario, they would be joining the All Star team as Astros rather than Expos or Orioles, respectively, as they were in 1971. Cesar Cedeno had gotten hot at that point, but he wasn't on the ballot. Joe Morgan and Bob Watson each had solid seasons and could have been considered, as well as a healthy Doug Rader on his way to an encore and a higher-spirited Jimmy Wynn living up to his reputation.

At the end of the season, the Houston Astros take the NL West divisional crown easily and prepare to host the Pittsburgh Pirates for the first two games of the National League Championship Series.

WHAT COULD HAVE BEEN:
THE POSTSEASON

Every baseball season winds down with its most exciting period: the postseason, when each qualifying team looks to bring home the hardware and call themselves champions. Clearly the 1971 Houston Astros were capable of reaching this point, so how would they have fared in October?

WhatIfSports.com is a website that simulates sports games and allows for composing different teams of different players to see what would have happened in such a game via an in-depth box score, line score, and play-by-play record that is generated within just a few seconds.

Before we begin, a couple of notes about how these simulations will be done:

1. The lineups used for the opposing team will be the same ones used by that team (The Pirates in the case of the NLCS) unless it is apparent that the team used a different lineup versus righty and lefty pitchers, in which case the appropriate lineup will be used.

2. Ace pitcher Larry Dierker was shut down in early-August, but given his confidence (Which he credits for being able to begin his career on his 18th birthday in 1964), and nearly two months of rest from early-August to early-October, it is likely that he could have come back to pitch in the postseason, particularly if he could get a shot like cortisone or rub a substance on his arm before his starts, which would have been at most four if he pitched in two games in

each series, if the Astros make it to the World Series. OR, just as a butterfly effect with the pitching rotation suddenly changed Doug Rader's health, the same might also happen with Dierker's, as now he would have more resources in a more first-class organization and more stable teammates in the rotation to take some of the pressure off him to win every start, and therefore he stays healthy. For the sake of the ideal for the Astros and the ballclub's fans, these simulations will assume Dierker to have been healthy all season, accumulating the stats mentioned in the previous chapter, going into the postseason.

Now, how would a National League Championship Series between the Houston Astros and Pittsburgh Pirates have ended? Could the Astros have won the pennant and advanced to the World Series? WhatIfSports. com has all the answers:

NATIONAL LEAGUE CHAMPIONSHIP SERIES

Game 1: Saturday, October 2 at 1 PM CT. Astrodome, Houston, TX

The Eighth Wonder of the World was the site of the beginning of the National League postseason in 1971, and the anxiously excited crowd could not wait to get inside the Astrodome to reverberate their loud cheering around the interior of the Dome, which was the only ballpark in baseball where this was possible because it was indoors. On a beautiful sunny, eighty-degree day in Houston, special tickets and scorecards were printed for the occasion, and Houston was proud to see their Dome, their Turf, their "Earthmen" grounds crew in orange spacesuits, their scoreboard, and most of all, their talented ballclub, viewed on the national stage.

Both the Pittsburgh Pirates and the Houston Astros started their long-time reliable ace pitchers on the mound: Steve Blass for the Pirates and Larry Dierker for the Astros.

The batting order for the Pirates was Dave Cash (2B), Richie Hebner (3B), Roberto Clemente (RF), Wilver Stargell (LF), Al Oliver (CF), Bob Robertson (1B), Manny Sanguillen (C), Jackie Hernandez (SS), and Steve Blass (P).

For the Astros, it was Sonny Jackson (SS), Joe Morgan (2B), Cesar Cedeno (CF), Jimmy Wynn (LF), Rusty Staub (RF), Bob Watson (1B), Doug Rader (3B), Jerry Grote (C), and Larry Dierker (P).

The National League umpire crew assigned to this series took their positions for Game 1 as follows: crew chief Tom Gorman (HP), Shag Crawford (1B), Lee Weyer (2B), Andy Olsen (3B), Dick Stello (LF), Satch Davidson (RF).

149

Dierker went the first three innings facing just three Pirate batters per, and it was during that time that the Orange Crush gave him an early lead. In the first inning, both Sonny Jackson and Cesar Cedeno hit singles, and Rusty Staub brought home Jackson with a base hit of his own. In the second inning, another Jackson single scored Doug Rader, and Jackson scored his second run of the game after Jimmy Wynn walked with the bases loaded. After three innings, the Astros led 3-0.

Cedeno collected his second hit of the game with an RBI single into right field to score Joe Morgan, and this set up the Toy Cannon Wynn to please the Astros fans with a two-run home run into left-center field. Wynn was able to do what he did best and do it in the postseason.

The Pirates' Jackie Hernandez doubled off the center field wall in the seventh to bring in Bob Robertson to avoid a shutout, but in the bottom half, Doug Rader lifted a fly ball deep enough to left field to allow Rusty Staub to tag up and score from third base and make the score 7-1.

If more insurance runs were needed, the eighth inning brought them as Joe Morgan scored on Staub's bases-loaded walk and Bob Watson singled in both Cedeno and Wynn. Jim Ray finished off the game by retiring all six Pirates in the last two innings, and by a score of 10-1, with nine of those ten runs coming with two outs and the tenth coming off a sacrifice fly that made the second out, Houston took an early series lead and gave the fans optimism that the same struggles their team had against the Bucs in the regular season would not continue in October. **HOU wins 10-1, HOU leads series 1-0**.

Game 2: Sunday, October 3 at 1 PM CT. Astrodome, Houston, TX

Astros' manager Mel McGaha kept the same lineup for Game 2 and started Don Wilson on the mound, but Pirates' manager Danny Murtaugh mixed up his lineup a little bit for Game 2. There were some similarities to the Game 1 lineup, but this time the lineup card said Dave Cash (2B), Gene Clines (CF), Roberto Clemente (RF), Wilver Stargell (LF), Bob Robertson (1B), Manny Sanguillen (C), Jose Pagan (3B), Jackie Hernandez (SS), and Dock Ellis (P). In Game 1, the Astros started the pitcher who was projected to start the All Star Game for the National League, and in Game 2, the Pirates would start the pitcher who did start the All Star Game.

Through five innings, both teams traded scoring chances and three-up, three-down innings no score. The Astros broke it open in the bottom of the sixth, beginning with a Joe Morgan walk and Cesar Cedeno fielder's choice and steal of second base. With a runner in scoring position, Jimmy Wynn's subsequent single drove home his fourth RBI of the series in just the first two games. Rusty Staub got on with a base hit, moving Wynn to third. After Bob Watson was retired, Doug Rader walked, and Jerry Grote hit another single through the left side of the infield, which scored Wynn and Staub. Don Wilson then flied out to end the inning and took the mound with a 3-0 advantage.

The Pirates threatened for the last time in the top of the seventh, but Manny Sanguillen was stranded ninety feet away. In the bottom half, Sonny Jackson greeted Pittsburgh reliever Nelson Briles with a leadoff double to set up Joe Morgan to move him to third with a groundout and Cesar Cedeno to single him home. Cedeno later stole second for the second time in the game, but with the score now 4-0, Houston was done scoring, and Don Wilson pitched perfect ball in the last two innings except for a two-out Jose Pagan single in the ninth. After Jackie Hernandez swung at strike three, Wilson completed a shutout to carry the Orange Crush into Pittsburgh only needing one more win for the pennant. **HOU wins 4-0, HOU leads series 2-0**.

Game 3: Tuesday, October 5 at 1:30 PM ET. Three Rivers Stadium, Pittsburgh, PA

An off day to travel was followed by Game 3 in Pittsburgh, with the Houston Astros only one win away from the franchise's first World Series berth. Mike Cuellar was slated to pitch for them, the first left-handed pitcher to start a game in the series, and after catcher Jerry Grote drove in two runs in Game 2, Mel McGaha decided to allow him to catch Game 3 as well, especially since he had a day of rest on the plane. McGaha's lineup remained the same. Danny Murtaugh, his team needing to win all three games in Pittsburgh, reverted to his Game 1 lineup against a lefty opposing pitcher and started Bob Johnson on the hill.

The Astros stranded Cesar Cedeno after a two-out walk in the top of the first inning, so when Roberto Clemente gave the Pittsburgh crowd and the Pirates early energy with a two-out solo home run in the bottom half, it gave them a 1-0 lead. Bob Watson responded quickly with the same effort the very next frame to tie it up, and even though the Orange Crush left the bases loaded in the third inning, he went opposite-field with another solo shot to put Houston in front 2-1.

Pitching for each side meandered its way through jams through the next few innings until Jack Billingham was called upon to pitch the eighth. With a one-run margin, he surrendered four straight singles, the last one coming from Clemente and scoring two runs to flip the tilt. Fred Gladding relieved Billingham and got three consecutive outs, but the damage was done, and the Astros went three-up, three-down in the ninth. In a game in which one player on each side batted in all his respective club's runs, the Pirates responded with their backs to the wall and scraped away a narrow win. **PIT wins 3-2, HOU leads 2-1**.

Game 4: Wednesday, October 6 at 1:30 PM ET. Three Rivers Stadium, Pittsburgh, PA

Danny Murtaugh retained the same batting order that won the previous day and brought back Game 1 starter Steve Blass to pitch. Mel McGaha kept his faith in the lineup card he presented, though he wrote in Johnny Edwards, who had won a pennant before, to bat in Jerry Grote's spot and catch righty Ken Forsch as the young hurler made his first postseason appearance. The more level-headed Edwards would surely help Forsch in a clinching game on the road.

The first three innings, save for Ken Forsch working around a two-out triple in the second inning, were quiet until the bottom of the third. A leadoff single by Dave Cash and a walk to Wilver Stargell two batters later put a runner in scoring position, and singles from Al Oliver and Bob Robertson scored both of them. Oliver came around when Manny Sanguillen reached on a Doug Rader error on a routine ground ball, uncharacteristic for him.

The next inning was the fourth, and during it, the Pirates scored their fourth run when Roberto Clemente brought home Steve Blass, who reached on a leadoff single.

The Astros threatened in the sixth when Johnny Edwards and pinch-hitter Manny Mota each singled and Sonny Jackson grounded out to advance them both, but Blass retired the next two batters to keep the score at 4-0.

Jackie Hernandez tacked on another tally by singling in Bob Robertson in the eighth inning to finish the Bucs' scoring at 5. When the Astros came up in the ninth, the top of the order was due up, and it looked promising when Sonny Jackson led off with an infield single and Joe Morgan clobbered a homer to right to put them on the board with two runs. However, the heart of the order was retired in order, and Pittsburgh had come back to tie the series at two games apiece, forcing a winner-take-all Game 5, the first in the history of the National League Championship Series. **PIT wins 5-2, series tied 2-2.**

Game 5: Thursday, October 7 at 1:30 PM ET. Three Rivers Stadium, Pittsburgh, PA

After the Astros took a commanding lead in the series in the Space City, they had failed to keep winning in the Steel City, and now they had to find a way to do just that or else go home.

Despite not winning the previous two games, the batting order for Houston was still executing well, so it did not change. Since the Pirates had won the past two games, they stuck with the same lineup as well. It was Dock Ellis' turn on the mound for Pittsburgh, and Houston skipper McGaha wrote in Larry Dierker to start. He had considered going with Wilson to save his ace for the first game of the World Series, but he decided to simply focus on the day at hand and make sure his team actually got to the Series first. This decision meant that the projected NL All

Star starter and the actual NL All Star starter would face each other in this pivotal Game 5.

As it turned out, Dierker got some help early that helped him relax. Joe Morgan walked and Cesar Cedeno singled, bringing up the Toy Cannon, who did what he does and smacked a long ball to dead center field. Singles by Rusty Staub and Bob Watson, followed by a walk to Doug Rader, loaded the bases for Johnny Edwards, who collected an RBI with a Texas-League base hit to plate Staub. Dierker and Sonny Jackson were put out to end the threat, but Houston had an early 4-0 cushion after a half-inning.

They would need it too. Richie Hebner, Roberto Clemente, and Wilver Stargell loaded the bases in the bottom half via two singles and a hit-by-pitch on the knee. Al Oliver flied to right field where Rusty Staub could not corral the ball and it went for a double, scoring Hebner and Clemente. Bob Robertson grounded out to bring home Stargell. Dierker got out of it before the Pirates could tie the game, and after one inning, every batter had a turn at bat (Sonny Jackson had two), and the score was 4-3 in favor of the Orange Crush.

The tides turned very quickly, as the second inning was three-up, three-down for both sides, but Stargell and Robertson collected extra-base hits in the third, a double and a triple, to tie the game. The Astros left two runners in scoring position in the fourth, but in the fifth, Bob Watson made up for it by going deeper than Jimmy Wynn's first inning blast to straight center for a two-run home run that allowed Staub to touch home before him after he had singled just off shortstop Jackie Hernandez's glove. The Astros led 6-4.

Clemente singled home Hernandez in the sixth to make it 6-5, so the scoring was high, but if either side wanted to win, their pitching would have to be the difference maker. Dierker left in the seventh, and George Culver came in and delivered two innings of one-hit shutout ball, even striking out two. The score remained the same in the ninth inning when Dave Giusti was given his biggest save situation of his career at this point:

allow no runs and you win the pennant. However, he would have to go through the heart of the "Lumber Company" Pirates' order to do it.

Clemente struck out swinging and Stargell grounded to Watson at first for two big sighs of relief. Oliver, a threat in the last two games, drew a walk, and Robertson singled to left-center to put Oliver on third. With the tying run ninety feet away and Manny Sanguillen stepping up, Giusti focused to deliver one last effort and struck Sanguillen out swinging. The Houston Astros were the 1971 National League Champions! **HOU wins 6-5, HOU wins series 3-2**.

After the celebration filled with orange and jubilance, the Astros needed to board the plane to arrive in their American League opponent's city, Baltimore.

Or is it that simple?

Since Mike Cuellar, who was with the 1971 Baltimore Orioles, is still an Astro in this case, that changes the pitching rotation for the American League Championship Series. The O's were too good to say they don't still win the AL Eastern division, but in a matchup versus the Western division winners, the Oakland A's, who wins now? Once again, Whatif-sports.com knows:

Game 1: OAK-3, BAL-0
Game 2: BAL-7, OAK-5
Game 3: BAL-1, OAK-0
Game 4: OAK-4, BAL-1
Game 5: OAK-10, BAL-2

Well, well, well, the Oakland A's are the American League Champions!

The Orioles' dynasty is cut a year shorter and the A's possibly begins a year sooner depending on how this World Series goes. Each league's counterculture team is representing them in the Fall Classic: Charlie O' Finley's A's and their modern Oakland Coliseum (Pre-Mount Davis) and green and yellow identity that showcases white spikes, yellow sanitary socks, and a grey-green tinted road uniform, referred to as "green mist," rather than the standard grey-blue tint most baseball teams use for their grey road uniforms; and Judge Roy Hofheinz's Astros and their Eighth Wonder of the World with a roof and artificial grass and "Orange Crush" uniforms that showcase orange as the primary accent color for the first time ever, as well as a chain-stitched "shooting star" home jersey wordmark and stirrups with an embroidered star on the side. This was just before each club began issuing double-knit polyester uniforms and before the A's mustaches, so that level of baseball tradition was still present as well. Rather than both teams having orange in their colors, we have a bright color contrast that even colorblind fans can enjoy. For traditionalists, this was sure to be a jarring sight. For youngsters and innovators, this World Series was set to be a scene to behold.

WORLD SERIES

Game 1: Saturday, October 9 at 1:00 PM PT. Oakland Coliseum, Oakland, CA

A sunny Oakland day with 60-degree temperatures greeted the teams and fans as they made the trek to Oakland Coliseum for the most anticipated event in sports: the World Series.

As Mel McGaha began to realize the opportunity and the pressure of putting together a World Series lineup, he decided that he would stick with what has worked, which for the Astros, was Sonny Jackson (SS), Joe Morgan (2B), Cesar Cedeno (CF), Jimmy Wynn (LF), Rusty Staub (RF), Bob Watson (1B), Doug Rader (3B), Jerry Grote (C), and Don Wilson (P). McGaha was most conflicted on whether to start the right-handed hitting Jerry Grote or the veteran Johnny Edwards behind the plate against lefty Vida Blue, but after remembering that the rest of the A's starting hurlers are righties, he elected to have the righty-hitting Grote catch, which would give the lefty-hitting Edwards a little more rest after finishing the NLCS behind the plate so that later in the series when they face righty pitchers, he would be ready.

Dick Williams, manager of the Oakland A's, also stuck with the lineup that got him to baseball's biggest stage, but he replaced the young Angel Mangual with the more seasoned Rick Monday since the former did not perform as well as Williams would have preferred in the LCS, and Monday did not get many opportunities in that series. His lineup spelled out Bert Campaneris (SS), Joe Rudi (LF), Reggie Jackson (RF), Tommy Davis (1B), Sal Bando (3B), Rick Monday (CF), Dave Duncan (C) Dick Green

157

(2B), and Vida Blue (P). The A's donned their gold alternate uniforms for Game 1.

The umpire crew for the World Series, as usual, was made up of six umpires, with three from the National League and three from the American League. In Game 1, they lined up in this way, alternating National and American League: crew chief Nestor Chylak (HP), Ed Sudol (1B), John Rice (2B), Ed Vargo (3B), Jim Odom (LF), John Kibler (RF). However, another umpire could have been considered as well. The first African American umpire in Major League Baseball Emmitt Ashford of the American League retired after calling the World Series between the Cincinnati Reds and Baltimore Orioles the year prior, but back in 1968, Oakland A's owner Charlie Finley requested that Ashford umpire behind the plate on Opening Day in the first game in Oakland because of his flamboyant mechanics and exciting demeanor on the field. Given that Astros owner Judge Hofheinz may have enjoyed the same thing, as well as the fact that commissioner Bowi Kuhn had hired Ashford as a public relations advisor in 1971, meaning Ashford was likely available, who says they don't ask Ashford to come out of retirement for one more Fall Classic?

The top of the Orange Crush order got started quickly as Sonny Jackson and Joe Morgan both walked to lead off the game, and Jackson stealing second base. They were left on when the heart of the order was put out by strikeout of Cesar Cedeno and popouts from Jimmy Wynn and Rusty Staub. Conversely, when Bert Campaneris singled to start the A's first batting inning, Joe Rudi immediately capitalized by bringing home Campy with a double to left field. Similarly, however, the A's 3-4-5 hitters were put out in succession, as Reggie Jackson and Tommy Davis struck out and Sal Bando fouled out to Jerry Grote along the backstop screen.

The next few innings were quiet with a couple small threats until Rudi knocked a homer barely over the right field wall just by the foul pole in the fifth inning. The A's had a 2-0 lead that Vida Blue comfortably held, with a Cesar Cedeno double in the sixth being his only blemish from that point, until the eighth frame. Manny Mota grounded out while pinch-hitting for Don Wilson, but Sonny Jackson lined a single to left and Joe Morgan reached on a Bert Campaneris error. Up came Cedeno, who with his second double of the day, chased home both Jackson and Morgan to tie the score at 2.

Jack Billingham pitched a perfect eighth inning of relief for Wilson and set the Astros up to take the lead in the ninth. Doug Rader walked with one out and Jerry Grote moved him to second with a groundout to Sal Bando at third. Norm Miller, the secret weapon, was called upon to hit for Billingham, and he lived up to his self-given nickname. He singled into right field, Reggie Jackson threw to catcher Dave Duncan at home, but while the throw was good, the Red Rooster maneuvered to avoid the tag and score. The Orange Crush took a 3-2 lead that their pitching secret weapon Dave Giusti could come along and save, and that is what he did by retiring the middle of the A's lineup in order. Don Wilson pitched seven inning of six-hit, two-run ball and surrendered a home run but struck out eight. Vida Blue went the distance for Oakland and gave up less hits but one more run, although one of those three runs was unearned. After it was all said and done, Houston had won its first-ever World Series game. **HOU wins 3-2, HOU leads series 1-0.**

Game 2: Sunday, October 10 at 1:00 PM PT. Oakland Coliseum, Oakland, CA

The second game of the Fall Classic would be played under another clear sky and around the same feeling as the day before at 58 degrees out. Each club had a little trouble scoring runs the day before, but Mel McGaha still remembered how his lineup had executed in the past, so he stuck with it to back up the left-handed Mike Cuellar on the mound, though Johnny Edwards would catch Cuellar and bat eighth to combat the A's right-handed starter. Despite the opposing southpaw, Dick Williams felt the same way about his batting order and kept it the same as well, and Catfish Hunter would be doing the starting pitching. The A's wore their home white uniforms.

Each side got a single in the first but nothing else. The A's got two more base hits in the second but a double play killed the opportunity.

The Astros got two walks in the third and a sacrifice bunt by Mike Cuellar but no execution there either. That's how it went until the bottom of the fourth. Sal Bando and Rick Monday each reached via single and walk, respectively, then Dave Duncan came up and crushed a three-run homer to left field to energize the rowdy Oakland crowd and put their A's in front 3-0.

The Astros' fifth spelled like their third, with two baserunners, namely Doug Rader and Johnny Edwards, aided by a sacrifice but the following two, Sonny Jackson and Joe Morgan, could not plate any runs. Jackson allowed Catfish Hunter to reach first base on an error, but he was stranded on second base.

In the seventh, Bob Watson and Doug Rader each collected singles, but Johnny Edwards flied out and pinch-hitter Manny Mota grounded into a double play.

The score remained 3-0 when Rusty Staub led off Houston's last chance inning with a solo blast down the right field line. After two groundouts to first baseman Tommy Davis, Johnny Edwards hit an infield single to Bert Campaneris, which sparked a pinch hitter from the Astros and a relief pitcher from the A's. Norm Miller stepped in against Rollie Fingers, hoping to come through in the same way he had the day before, but this time Fingers froze him on the third strike, and the A's had now won their first World Series game for Oakland. **OAK wins 3-1, series tied 1-1**.

Game 3: Tuesday, October 12 at 1 PM CT. Astrodome, Houston, TX

As the Houston Astros descended back into town on the plane, seeing the Astrodome beneath them, the team remembered their home-field advantage and how tough it was for other clubs who were not used to playing in the Dome regularly to adjust. The Oakland A's from the American League did not play against any opponent during the regular season with an indoor ballpark or an all-artificial turf field (The White Sox had an infield of "Sox Sod," but they could not afford the outfield), and there were only three members of the A's that played in the Dome at the 1968

MLB All Star Game: Bert Campaneris, Rick Monday, and Blue Moon Odom. Therefore, since the Astros had already won one game in Oakland, they felt confident and hopeful that they could sweep the three games in Houston and end the series at Dome Sweet Dome and satisfy their loyal fans with a championship win that they could witness.

On this day, it was 79 degrees and sunny, but even if it had been raining hard, baseball would still be played in the one Major League city that could host a game under those conditions. Under the roof of the Eighth Wonder of the World, Game 3 of the 1971 World Series was being praised as a historic day in baseball history. Each ballclub wanted to perform well on the big stage, so each manager meticulously carved out their lineup cards, and Oakland skipper Dick Williams devised this: Bert Campaneris (SS), Rick Monday (CF), Reggie Jackson (RF), Mike Epstein (1B), Sal Bando (3B), Angel Mangual (LF), Gene Tenace (C), Dick Green (2B), and Diego Segui (P). They wore the all-gold uniform to coincide with the series moving to Houston.

Mel McGaha felt best with the same lineup as he believed in his team to succeed in the Astrodome as well. He also believed in the young yet competitive Ken Forsch to deliver a great game on the mound, so it was number 43 that was under the "P" for pitcher on the Astrodome scoreboard.

A quiet first inning fed into a productive second inning for the A's. Mike Epstein walked, Sal Bando lined out, Angel Mangual singled to move Epstein to second, and Gene Tenace grounded into a fielder's choice when the Astros middle infield got one out at second but not Tenace at first. This moved Epstein to third, where he did not stay for long as Dick Green singled to left field to score him and grab a one-run lead.

The Orange Crush had to come around at some point in this first World Series game in the Astrodome, and in the third inning they did. Doug Rader and Johnny Edwards led off with singles, and after Ken Forsch grounded back to Diego Segui who threw to second for one out, Sonny Jackson walked to load the bases for Joe Morgan. Morgan also drew a walk, and that scored Rader. Cesar Cedeno lined out to Bert Campaneris at shortstop, but then the Toy Cannon Jimmy Wynn gave the Houston crowd what they had been waiting for: a home run in the World Series. He took Segui deep, the home run spectacular on the AstroLite scoreboard went off for an Astros home run in the World Series for the first time, and Forsch helped himself by touching home with one of the four runs that was added to the Astros' score after the grand slam that made the score 5-1.

Forsch quickly undid his progress by surrendering a Sal Bando double and a wild pitch to move him to third, where he easily tagged up and scored from when Angel Mangual flied to deep left. The remainder of the fourth was easy, and so was the top of the fifth. Forsch stepped back into the batter's box in the bottom of the frame, intent on putting himself back in position to win this game. He did his part by blooping a single to right-center, and he stole second on the same pitch Sonny Jackson struck out swinging on. Joe Morgan walked, and Cesar Cedeno beat out an infield hit to Bert Campaneris. After Jimmy Wynn went down swinging, Rusty Staub singled in both Forsch and Morgan to make the score 7-2, then Bob Watson became the beneficiary of a Campaneris error that put the Bull on first and Cedeno on the board with the Astros' eighth run. Segui was replaced by Darold Knowles in the sixth. The Orange Crush was indeed in the building.

Staub helped Forsch again in the seventh after Cedeno and Wynn collected base hits with a sacrifice fly to right-center, and Cedeno scored when Rick Monday was late with his throw home to Gene Tenace. This knocked Knowles out of the ballgame to be replaced by Bob Locker.

The "Swinging A's," while down, were not yet out, however, as two walks to Reggie Jackson and Mike Epstein meant that Sal Bando's subsequent double brought home Jackson and chased Ken Forsch out of the game in the eighth inning. Jack Billingham did what any reliever is supposed to do—get the first batter you face out—by getting Angel Mangual to fly out, but Gene Tenace then reached on an infield single to Doug Rader at third, and Epstein scored. The game was now at a 9-4 split.

The bottom of the eighth was three-up, three-down for Houston except for a pinch-hit home run from longtime franchise-favorite Bob Aspromonte to make the score 10-4. Astros closer Dave Giusti was brought on in the ninth inning with his usual save situation, and he easily worked around a one-out walk to Rick Monday to get Reggie Jackson via flyout and Mike Epstein on a swing and a miss. For the first time ever, Houston fans were cheering a World Series game victory in their own city. **HOU wins 10-4, HOU leads series 2-1**.

Game 4: Wednesday, October 13 at 7:15 PM CT. Astrodome, Houston, TX

Another big milestone of this World Series was that Game 4 would be the first time a Series game would be played at night. Perhaps MLB was hoping that the game would be played in an outdoor venue so the night sky could be seen, but nonetheless, more history was being made in this game.

With the amazing Vida Blue returning to pitch, Dick Williams left his lineup, clad in their "green mist" road grey uniforms, the way it was, sure that any lineup combination of his could score one or two runs, which would be enough for Blue. Mel McGaha believed the same about his batting order, whether Larry Dierker or Don Wilson got the ball. It was Dierker's turn, but Wilson was also rested enough, and McGaha knew it would be a great story if Dierker pitched–and won–the clinching game of the World Series in the Dome after his phenomenal season and his status as franchise player. If Wilson pitched this day and won, it would set that up. If he lost, McGaha determined that Dierker would pitch anyways. He penciled in number 40, Don Wilson, as his starter.

Wilson was greeted by Bert Campaneris to start the game with a lead-off single, but he was soon greeted by the arm of Johnny Edwards, who gunned down Campy trying to steal second base. The next two A's batters retired, and Sonny Jackson gave Vida Blue the same greeting in the bottom of the first. Joe Morgan moved Jackson over to second, but that didn't keep him from stealing third. After Cesar Cedeno took ball four, he stole second to put two runs in scoring position with one out. Jimmy Wynn hit a laser into left field for a two-RBI double, then Rusty Staub singled up the middle to score Wynn. The Astros had a 3-0 lead.

Dick Green led off the third with an infield hit to shortstop, and a Vida Blue sacrifice and Joe Morgan error pushed Green to second, then third. After Rick Monday's fly ball wasn't quite deep enough to plate Green, Reggie Jackson hit another infield single to Sonny Jackson, and the A's were on the board. Bob Watson got that run back in the fourth with a solo home run down the left field line, but two innings later Angel Mangual singled home Reggie Jackson to make the score 4-2. Sal Bando replicated that effort in the eighth with a base hit that scored Rick Monday. Don Wilson finished what he started, and after a three-up, three-down ninth inning, he had his second win of the Series. As had been the case so often in 1971, the Astros played to a one-run final score. The Orange Crush had won it in this case and was now one win away from baseball immortality. **HOU wins 4-3, HOU leads series 3-1.**

Game 5: Thursday, October 14 at 1 PM CT. Astrodome, Houston, TX

Houstonians woke up early on yet another bright, sunny day that would top out at 83 degrees, even though the Astros played a night game the night before, because they were anxious to either turn on the radio, television, or ignition of their vehicles as they made their way to the Astrodome. The entire city was full of excitement knowing that this could be the day that their Houston Astros win the World Series. School-aged kids tried to sneak radios into school to listen quietly in class or with friends at lunch. They biked to school knowing that they would want to rush home immediately after class to get home and finish watching or listening to World Series Game 5, being played right in their town. Maybe some teachers even brought their radios or televisions to class. Many working men and women across the metropolitan area felt similarly.

In the Oakland A's clubhouse, the team knew they had no more room for mistakes. Dick Williams sat Angel Mangual and Gene Tenace and replaced them with Joe Rudi and Dave Duncan, taking their place both in field position and batting slot. In the same grey uniform as yesterday, Catfish Hunter would be going up against Larry Dierker, as Mel McGaha's decision on that had been made the day before. He stuck with the same lineup. The team was ecstatic to get on the field and win the biggest game of their careers, and they were ready.

Larry Dierker held the A's hitless for the first two innings, and in the third when he gave up his first hit (To pitcher Catfish Hunter), his team responded in the bottom of the inning by scoring a run. Johnny Edwards reached via single and was put out at second when Dierker grounded into a fielder's choice. Two more base hits by Sonny Jackson and Joe Morgan pushed Dierker around the bases to score the game's first run and help Dierker aid his own cause.

Doug Rader added another run in the fourth inning when he also hit into a fielder's choice that retired Bob Watson but allowed Rusty Staub to come home. The top of the order tallied a third run in the fifth when Sonny Jackson singled and Joe Morgan doubled to left field, bringing around Jackson. In the sixth, the A's got their second hit from Bert Campaneris, but for the fourth consecutive inning, the Orange Crush pushed one across. Johnny Edwards blooped a double into left-center field to score Rusty Staub, who had led off the inning with a walk, to make the score 4-0. The butterflies were intensifying in the Dome and throughout the city.

Larry Dierker's entire career, from striking out Willie Mays in his big league debut on his 18th birthday to multiple close calls with no-hitters to his career year in 1969 to his even better start to the 1971 season, culminated in this one Game 5 of the computer-generated 1971 World Series.

Dierker was left in to finish the game in the ninth after he had already thrown eight strong innings, so he, skipper McGaha, catcher Edwards, and the rest of the Astros and Houston figured, what's one more inning when you have a four-run lead, and this could win you the World Series? He got Rick Monday to go down whiffing. Reggie Jackson singled, and Mike Epstein flied out to Jimmy Wynn in shallow left field for two outs. Sal Bando grounded a single to left, and pitching coach, Jim Owens, who had predicted that Dierker would win 25 games back in May, went out to visit his ace and relax him, and give closer Dave Giusti time to warm up in case he was needed. Joe Rudi proved that the A's were not going down easily, as with a single to right, Reggie Jackson scored and the A's were on the board, with the score now being 4-1. Now Dave Duncan stepped up as the tying run. Dierker put out of his head the runners on first and second and the run he had just given up and put all his focus on getting Duncan out. He got the Oakland catcher to ground a ball to Sonny Jackson at shortstop, who gathered himself to throw the ball to Bob Watson, and he cleanly caught the Sports Illustrated cover star's throw for the final out. **HOU wins 4-1, HOU wins series 4-1**.

THE HOUSTON ASTROS WERE THE 1971 WORLD SERIES CHAMPIONS!

Most of the Orange Crush batters were sufficient except for Jimmy Wynn (.167) and Bob Watson (.158), though they each lit up the Astro-Lite with home runs. Doug Rader (.235), Joe Morgan (.250), Sonny Jackson (.263), and Cesar Cedeno (.263) made timely contributions, as did Johnny Edwards (.333) in four games behind the plate catching the Astros pitching. Mike Cuellar, Ken Forsch, and Larry Dierker each made one start, with Cuellar falling on hard luck in his outing, Forsch winning his, and Dierker carrying Houston to the promise land by winning the World Series-clinching game of Astro fans' dreams. Dave Giusti collected two saves to shut down the opposition late in the game. Don Wilson started twice, winning both, one of them being a complete game, and striking out 14 with an ERA of 2.29. The World Series Most Valuable Player Award, however, easily went to Rusty Staub. He batted .353 while scoring three runs and batting in five. Two of his hits were a double and a home run.

What if all of this—the better front office organization, the smarter general manager, the retention of young and strong talent, the optimism in the clubhouse, and of course, the winning on the field—had actually happened? Houston would not have had to wait until 1980, sixteen years after the founding of the franchise, to see postseason baseball. Neither would the fans have needed to wait until 2005 for the team's first pennant or 2017 for its first World Series title. The core of Wynn, Morgan (No infamous Reds trade!), Watson, Rader, Cedeno, Staub, Dierker, Wilson, and Cuellar may have played their entire careers in Houston, or at least have played their prime for the Astros rather than using it elsewhere. Morgan would have an Astros cap on his Hall of Fame plaque in Cooperstown, making him the first player to be inducted as an Astro. Cedeno likely joins him soon after, and the Hall of Fame cases for players such as Dierker, Cuellar, Wynn, and others on the Astros are dwelled upon by writers and fans who witnessed the legendary Orange Crush. Dierker, having now been the starting and winning pitcher in the team's World Series-winning game, would have that to go along with the rest of his pitching career, his broadcasting experience in the 1980's, and his stint as Astros manager from 1997 to 2001 to further stamp his title as Mr. Astro. New Orleans and its Superdome may have been more seriously considered for expansion in the 1970's than they were, due to the success and popularity of the nearby Astros. Judge Hofheinz's financial troubles would have been largely alleviated, if not avoided, due to more fans coming out to the Astrodome and the AstroDomain for winning baseball in addition to the Eighth Wonder of the World. The Orange Crush Houston Astros would be spoken of in the same breath as the Lumber Company Pittsburgh Pirates, Swinging Oakland A's, Big Red Machine Cincinnati Reds, and Baltimore Orioles as MLB dynasties of the 1970's.

The players and fans would not have to pine over the question of what could have been, but rather they would remember the 1971 team forever. They would not be the Neglected Houston Astros of 1971.

.

THE 1971 HOUSTON ASTROS

Pitchers

42 Jack Billingham, 10-16, 3.39 ERA

Believed to be a distant cousin of Christy Mathewson, Jack Billingham was included in the most infamous trade in Astros history that also sent Joe Morgan to the Cincinnati Reds in November of 1971. Billingham became a stalwart of the Reds' rotation and helped the Big Red Machine to back-to-back World Series titles in 1975 and 1976. He later pitched two seasons for the Detroit Tigers and one with the Boston Red Sox before retiring from pitching in 1980. Seven years later he began coaching for three Astros' minor league teams from 1987 to 2003.

36 Wade Blasingame, 9-11, 4.60 ERA

Wade Blasingame retired after pitching for the New York Yankees in 1972. In 1985, he was inducted into the Fresno County Athletic Hall of Fame. After his baseball career, he found residences in Marietta, Georgia during winter and Anchorage, Alaska during summer, and began working in the industry of oil and gasoline pipelines. He eventually returned to baseball by joining the American Legion Baseball Board of Directors.

41 Ron Cook, 0-4, 4.91 ERA

While Ron Cook pitched in six games for the Astros in 1971, an injury in Venezuela during winter ball the offseason prior prevented his career from going any further.

39 George Culver, 5-8, 2.64 ERA

George Culver pitched one more season in Houston in 1972 before moving on to the Dodgers, and then to the Phillies. Tommy John believes that Culver being placed on waivers during 1973 was the reason the Dodgers missed the postseason. In 1975, he traveled abroad to play for the Nippon-Ham fighters in Japan. His last two big league teams were the organizations that he coached in after his pitching career and until 2010. He remains active in the Bakersfield, California, community in several ways, especially when baseball is involved.

49 Larry Dierker, 12-6, 2.72 ERA

Larry Dierker adapted his pitching motion in 1972 to ease his elbow, but that only aggravated his shoulder, and he would pitch with that pain for the remainder of his career. It was also in 1972 when, as Houston Astros player representative, Dierker was outspoken about clarifying what MLB players were striving for during the preseason strike, which was not merely more money, but more security regarding retirement pensions and medical benefits. He threw a no-hitter on July 9, 1976, against the Montreal Expos, and finished his career with 30 games for the St. Louis Cardinals in 1977. He returned to the Astros organization as director of community relations and ticket sales during the late-70's. For most of the 1980's and 1990's, Dierker served as a broadcaster for the Astros, and his insights inspired the organization to hire him to be the manager in 1997. In 1998 he led the Astros to 102 wins, a franchise record for 20 years until the 2018 club broke it, and he was awarded the Manager of the Year honor. Dierker carried the club into the next century before stepping down in 2001. He wrote two books after his playing career, *This Ain't Brain Surgery: How to Win the Pennant Without Losing Your Mind,* and *My Team: Choosing My Dream Team from My Forty Years in Baseball.* His number was retired by the Astros in 2002, and he was inducted into the Astros Hall of Fame as part of its inaugural class in 2019. Dierker currently runs a youth baseball division of the suburban Houston charity Cy-Hope called Dierker's Champs.

43 Ken Forsch, 8-8, 2.53 ERA

Ken Forsch pitched in the rotation and out of the bullpen interchangeably throughout his time in Houston and was selected as an All Star in 1976 and in 1981 when he was with the California Angels. He pitched a no-hitter on April 7, 1979, to add to his brother Bob, who make up the only brother combination to each pitch no-hitters in the Major Leagues. He pitched for the Angels until a dislocated shoulder eventually forced him into retirement in 1986. Forsch spent time in real estate and speaking for the Angels and was even in the Angels' front office when the club won the World Series in 2002. He left that position of director of player development in 2011.

48 Fred Gladding, 4-5, 2.10 ERA

Fred Gladding retired from pitching in June 1973 with the highest pitching winning percentage in Tigers' history among pitchers with over 200 games pitched. In 1969 he led the National League in saves the first year the stat was created. He joined the Tigers as a pitching coach for three seasons beginning in 1976. He holds the lowest non-zero career batting average in baseball history with a .016 clip, thanks to a base hit in New York on July 30, 1969, with the Astros. Gladding died on May 21, 2015, at age seventy-eight.

52 Bill Greif, 1-1, 5.06 ERA

Most of Bill Greif's career was spent with the San Diego Padres from 1972 to 1976, and he was the team's Opening Day starter in 1974. He tried catching on with a brief stint with the St. Louis Cardinals in 1976 and in 1978 with the Tidewater Tides, affiliate of the New York Mets, but he only lasted part of a season in St. Louis and three games in Norfolk. A highlight of his career was picking off Lou Brock.

38 Tom Griffin, 0-6, 4.78 ERA

Tom Griffin left the Astros in 1976 and made the rounds in California with stops in San Diego, Anaheim, and San Francisco, before rounding out his career in Pittsburgh in 1982. He never could match the potential he revealed for himself during his rookie season in 1969, but he still put up a solid Major League career.

35 Skip Guinn, 0-0, 0.00 ERA

Skip Guinn pitched in three big league seasons: for the Atlanta Braves in 1968 and the Astros in 1969 and 1971. He was included in the reworked Rusty Staub trade after Donn Clendenon refused to report to play for the Astros. His maternal grandson is Kyle Harrison, who made his big league debut with the Giants in 2023.

46 Buddy Harris, 1-1, 6.46

Buddy Harris pitched two seasons in Houston and did not see the big leagues again after 1971. After the 1972 season, he and Rich Chiles were traded to the New York Mets for Tommie Agee. Arm trouble brought about his retirement after 1973. He went back to the Philadelphia area and taught math and history while he owned a deli restaurant. Harris died on November 5, 2022, at age seventy-three.

23 Denny Lemaster, 0-2, 3.45 ERA

Denny Lemaster was sold to the Montreal Expos for the 1972 season, which turned out to be his last. He turned to his interest of the outdoors and turned fishing and hunting into semi-steady work, entering tournaments such as one in Georgia that inspired him to take up residence in the Peach State and take up woodworking. Lemaster died on July 24, 2024, at age eighty-five.

45 Jim Ray, 10-4, 2.12 ERA

Jim Ray, nicknamed the "Ray Gun," pitched for the Astros until 1973, then spent a season with the Detroit Tigers to finish off his underrated relief career. He died on May 26, 2005 at age sixty.

50 J.R. Richard, 2-1, 3.43 ERA

As good as J.R. Richard was in his four games in 1971, he improved every year, becoming a full-time starter in 1975 and striking out 300 batters in 1978. 1980 proved to be his best season, garnering a 10-4 record with 115 strikeouts and a 1.96 ERA during the first half of the season and earning the starting pitcher role in that year's All Star Game. Meanwhile, his arm was going numb often during starts, limiting how far into games he could pitch, and on July 30, he had a major stroke while throwing in the Astrodome outfield before a game. This ended his career, and began some sorrow from members of the Astros' organization who believed Richard's arm complaints were him trying to get out of playing. Later in life, he lost $300,000 in an oil scam and was left homeless in Houston until a church he had begun work with and the Astros found out and helped him out of poverty. Richard was inducted into the Astros Hall of Fame in 2019 and died on August 4, 2021, at age seventy-one.

37 Scipio Spinks, 1-0, 3.68

Scipio Spinks was traded to the St. Louis Cardinals in April 1972, where he rivaled some of the best pitchers in the league and was fast enough to pinch-run until a collision at home plate tore ligaments in his right knee, affecting the remainder of his career. He has scouted for the Padres, Astros, and Diamondbacks organizations and is currently the manager of the University of Houston-Downtown Gators club baseball team.

40 Don Wilson, 16-10, 2.45 ERA

Don Wilson was the Astros' Opening Day starter in 1972, a season in which he closely replicated his career-year of 1971, His next two seasons, which ended up being his last two seasons, saw him tail off a little bit, but he still managed some dominating outings before 1974 was finished. On January 5, 1975, Wilson, twenty-nine, and his son Alexander, five, were found dead, Don in his car and Alex in his bedroom. Don had left the engine running in his car, and the fumes traveled up to Alex's room, where the fumes poisoned him as well. Mystery still surrounds Wilson's death, but the Astros continue to recognize him, wearing a patch for him in 1975 with his number on it, which was retired by the team during the same season. Wilson was inducted into the Astros Hall of Fame in 2019.

31 Larry Yount, 0-0, 0.00 ERA

After one credited game when he did not face a batter due to a stiff arm, Larry Yount never played in another Major League game, despite trying to make it back through the minor leagues. He was traded to the Milwaukee Brewers in 1974, where he was with his younger brother Robin during Spring Training, but he could not hold on, and resorted to real estate in Arizona. Robin, meanwhile, became an All Star shortstop and was inducted into the National Baseball Hall of Fame in 1999.

Catchers

7 Johnny Edwards, .233, 1 HR, 23 RBI

Edwards continued to catch for the Astros until his retirement in 1974. Because of his education from Ohio State University and his application of his degree during off seasons, he was well-prepared to take on work at an ironworks company in Houston after he retired, and he climbed up the chain of command to eventually become a plant manager. He retired in 2002.

8, Jack Hiatt, .276, 1 HR, 16 RBI

Jack Hiatt finished his career in 1972 with the California Angels, and managed in the Cubs, Angels, Astros, and Giants organizations. He also served as the director of player development for the Giants, a position he retired from in 2007 after sixteen years.

10, Larry Howard, .234, 2 HR, 14 RBI

Larry Howard played one more season for the Astros in 1972 before being traded to the Atlanta Braves for 1973, where his career ended. He died on May 11, 2019, at age seventy-three.

First Basemen

33 John Mayberry, .182, 7 HR, 14 RBI

John Mayberry was traded to the Kansas City Royals after the 1971 season in one of Spec Richardson's disastrous trades. As soon as 1972, he batted .298 and hit 25 home runs while bringing in 100 runs. These numbers became typical for him, and in 1975, he finished second in American League MVP voting, also making the All Star team in the two seasons prior. He finished up his career after five years with the Toronto Blue Jays and part of a season with the New York Yankees. After his retirement in 1982, Mayberry coached in the Blue Jays and Royals organizations, worked in the Royals Community Affairs Department, and was inducted into the Royals Hall of Fame in 1996.

11 Denis Menke, .246, 1 HR, 43 RBI

Denis Menke, a shortstop for most of his career, was traded to the Cincinnati Reds on November 29, 1971, and he played two seasons with the Reds, including during the 1972 World Series. He returned to Houston in 1974, where he ended his career in July of that year. Following his playing career, he began coaching in the Toronto Blue Jays organization, and he worked his way up to the big league club before also coaching for the Astros, Philadelphia Phillies, and Reds. Menke died on December 1, 2020, at age eighty.

27 Bob Watson, .288, 9 HR, 67 RBI

The "Bull" hit .300 in four seasons in Houston and hit for the cycle in 1977, the same season he appeared in the movie *The Bad News Bears in Breaking Training* in a cameo role. He made the National League All Star team in 1973 and 1975, and he also scored baseball's one millionth run in 1975. In 1979, with the Boston Red Sox, Watson hit for the cycle again, making him the first player to do so in both leagues. After stints with the New York Yankees and Atlanta Braves, he retired in 1984 and became the hitting coach for the Oakland A's. He became the second black general manager in MLB history in 1989 when the Astros hired him to fill the role, which he later also filled with the Yankees during their late-90's dynasty. Watson worked for USA Baseball and the Baseball Assistance Team. He survived prostate cancer in 1994 but succumbed to kidney disease on May 14, 2020, at age seventy-four.

Second Basemen
14 Marty Martinez, .288, 0 HR, 4 RBI

Marty Martinez spent 1972 with three teams: the St. Louis Cardinals, Oakland A's, and Texas Rangers, the latter being the organization he would begin his managing career with. After two seasons in the Rangers' double-A affiliate Tulsa Drillers, he joined the Seattle Mariners organization and served as the big league club's interim manager for one game in 1986. Martinez died on March 8, 2007, at age sixty-five.

18 Joe Morgan, .256, 13 HR, 56 RBI

The "Little General" was the centerpiece in the Astros' package to the Cincinnati Reds on November 29, 1971. Rather than Spec Richardson either fire Harry Walker or trade Jimmy Wynn, he believed Morgan was a bad influence on Wynn, so he traded Morgan. Because of Morgan's success in leading the Big Red Machine to back-to-back World Series titles and MVP awards, it is believed that this trade jumpstarted the Big Red Machine. He rejoined the Astros in 1980 when they won the National League West division for the first time. He then spent two seasons with the San Francisco Giants and one apiece with the Philadelphia Phillies and Oakland A's. Morgan began a lustrous broadcasting career after he retired from playing but was recognized for his on-field ability with a 1990 induction into the National Baseball Hall of Fame. He is also in both the Cincinnati Reds and Houston Astros Halls of Fame. Morgan died on October 11, 2020, at age seventy-seven.

19 Derrel Thomas, .000, 0 HR, 0 RBI

After making his big league debut as a September call-up with the Astros in 1971, Derrel Thomas was traded to the San Diego Padres after the season, and spent time with the San Francisco Giants, Los Angeles Dodgers, Montreal Expos, California Angels, and Philadelphia Phillies before retiring in 1985. He won the 1981 World Series with the Dodgers. Thomas later managed an independent league team and a high school team.

Third Basemen
12 Doug Rader, .244, 12 HR, 56 RBI

The "Red Rooster" won three more Gold Glove awards with the Astros from 1972 to 1974, making that five consecutive that he would win. Rader was traded to the San Diego Padres for the 1976 season and was purchased by the Toronto Blue Jays midway through the 1977 season, which was his last. In 1979, he joined the Padres as a coach and was given the reins of the triple-A Hawaii Islanders in 1980. Throughout the 1980's, he managed the Texas Rangers and the California Angels, while also serving as interim manager for the Chicago White Sox for two games in 1986. He retired from coaching after coaching for the expansion Florida Marlins for the franchise's first two seasons.

Shortstops
16 Ray Busse, .147, 0 HR, 4 RBI

Ray Busse was traded to the St. Louis Cardinals in 1972, but only played there in 1973 and was dealt back to Houston the next season, where his career ended in 1974.

15, Roger Metzger, .235, 0 HR, 26 RBI

Roger Metzger remained the Astros' starting shortstop until 1976, leading the National League in doubles in 1971 and 1973. He was sold to the San Francisco Giants in 1978, but a table-saw accident left him without the tips of four fingers on his right hand, and his career ended in

1980, though the Giants retained him as a coach for the remainder of the 1980 season.

Outfielders
22 Jesus Alou, .279, 2 HR, 40 RBI

Jesus Alou was traded to the Oakland A's in 1973, winning two World Series there, but after spending a season with the New York Mets, found his way back to Houston for two seasons in 1978 and 1979. His post-playing career consisted of a scouting role for the Montreal Expos, an executive position with the Florida Marlins, and a part-time ambassador for the Boston Red Sox until 2020. Alou died on March 10, 2023, at age eighty.

28, Cesar Cedeno, .264, 10 HR, 81 RBI

Cesar Cedeno began to reach his full potential in 1972 and 1973 with breakout seasons that earned him the nickname "Superbaby." His performance tailed off after a domestic incident during the offseason of 1973 and injuries began plaguing him, but he still made four All Star teams and won five straight Gold Gloves from 1972 to 1976. Cedeno began making the rounds in 1982, first in three seasons with the Cincinnati Reds and one season apiece with the St. Louis Cardinals and Los Angeles Dodgers. He later coached in the Washington Nationals and Astros organizations. Cedeno was inducted into the Astros Hall of Fame in 2020.

Rich Chiles, .227, 2 HR, 15 RBI

Rich Chiles played two more seasons with the Astros in 1972 and in 1976, spending time with the New York Mets in between and the Minnesota Twins afterwards. He coached for the University of California, Davis baseball team and the Carolina Mudcats, and scouted for the San Diego Padres and Milwaukee Brewers.

20 Cesar Geronimo, .220, 1 HR, 6 RBI

Cesar Geronimo was traded to the Cincinnati Reds after the 1971 season, where he won two World Series and four straight Gold Glove awards with the Big Red Machine. He ended his career with three seasons with the Kansas City Royals and was inducted into the Cincinnati Reds Hall of Fame in 2008.

21 Norm Miller, .257, 2 HR, 10 RBI

The "Secret Weapon" remained with the Astros until he was traded to Atlanta in 1973. He saw Hank Aaron's 715th home run live and, like Aaron, left the Braves after the 1974 season. Miller returned to Houston where he served in a front office role with the Astros.

17 Jay Schlueter, .333, 0 HR, 0 RBI

Jay Schlueter never appeared in the Majors again after 1971 but was traded to the Baltimore Orioles in 1974. After his minor league career was finished, he coached baseball in Arizona and New Mexico and became a real estate broker. Schlueter died on May 13, 2010, at age sixty.

24 Jimmy Wynn, .203, 7 HR, 45 RBI

The "Toy Cannon" rebounded from his 1971 slump to play two more solid seasons in Houston before being traded to the Los Angeles Dodgers, where he made two All Star teams and won the pennant in 1974. Wynn finished his career with the Atlanta Braves, New York Yankees, and Milwaukee Brewers and retired after 1977. He later served as a broadcaster and community outreach executive for the Astros. His number was retired by the Astros in 2005 and he was indicted into the Astros Hall of Fame in 2019. Wynn died on March 26, 2020, at age seventy-eight.

Manager
25 Harry Walker

"The Hat" was fired from the Astros in August of 1972, and he returned to the team he played the most with, the St. Louis Cardinals, to become a hitting instructor. In 1979 he helped begin the baseball program at the University of Alabama at Birmingham by serving as the team's first manager, and his number 32 was later retired by the program. He was inducted into the Alabama Sports Hall of Fame in 1978. Walker died on August 8, 1999, at age eighty.

Coaches
4 Buddy Hancken

Buddy Hancken served as both a coach and a member of the front office for the Astros in 1971 and returned to the role in 1991 for two years. He died on February 15, 2007, at age ninety-two.

5 Jim Owens

Former Phillies and Astros pitcher Jim Owens held the job of pitching coach for the Astros until 1972. He never took on another baseball job, rather getting a job with an oil drilling company. Owens was added to the Syracuse Chiefs Wall of Fame in 2005. He was known to not sign many autographs later in his life, including requests received through the mail. Owens died on September 8, 2020, at age eighty.

3 Hub Kittle

Hub Kittle became the Astros' pitching coach in 1973 and left in 1976 to join the Cardinals, where he was a minor league manager, roving pitching instructor, and Major League pitching coach. He won the World Series with the Cardinals in 1982. He maintained a part-time pitching instructor job with the Seattle Mariners later in his life until he died on February 10, 2004, at age eighty-six.

2 Salty Parker

Salty Parker bridged the gap between managers after Harry Walker was fired in 1972 for one game in August, which the team won. He was fired after the season and went on to coach for the California Angels, San Francisco Giants, and Seattle Mariners in varying capacities. He was indicted into the Texas Baseball Hall of Fame in 1991, and died on July 27, 1992, at age eighty.

Broadcasters

Gene Elston, KPRC-Radio, KTRK-TV

Gene Elston began broadcasting Houston Buffs games on the radio in 1961 and took the job for the Colt 45s when the National League expanded to Houston. He held his position for the Astros until 1986, and he took a position of calling national broadcasts in 1987. Elston was known for being reserved in his manner of calling the game. His accolades include induction into the Texas Baseball Hall of Fame in 1993 and the Texas Radio Hall of Fame in 2002, and the Ford C. Frick Award in 2006. Elston died on September 5, 2015, at age ninety-three.

Loel Passe, KPRC-Radio, KTRK-TV

Loel Passe began broadcasting Houston Buffs games in 1950, and he shifted into the same role for the Houston Major League club in 1962. Between 1962 and the time Passe left the team in 1976, he never missed a game and served as the color commentator for Gene Elston, as he differed from Elston's persona with an exciting, flamboyant way of almost cheering on the team from the microphone. Passe took a job with a freight company after his broadcasting days and he died on July 15, 1997, at age eighty. He was posthumously inducted into the Texas Radio Hall of Fame.

Rene Cardenas, Spanish Broadcast

Rene Cardenas was hired by the Houston Colt 45s to broadcast the games in Spanish, and he did so until the Spanish broadcasts were cancelled in 1975. After spending time with the Texas Rangers and Los Angeles Dodgers, he returned to the Astros in 2007. Cardenas was inducted into the Astros Hall of Fame in 2024.

Other Broadcasters

Ron Franklin: KHOU-TV
Ted Shaw and Bill Enis: KPRC-TV
Dan Lovett: KTRK-TV

Owner
Judge Roy M. Hofheinz

Before joining the Houston Sports Association to bring Major League Baseball to Houston, Judge Hofheinz served in the Texas House of Representatives as well as serving as the County Judge of Harris County and Mayor of Houston. As the 1970's went along, he began to have financial difficulty as the glamor of the Astrodome was beginning to fade and the team was not stirring enough interest to maintain the high attendance numbers. Hofheinz began to sell off parts of the Astrodomain such as AstroWorld and the AstroWorld Hotel, and the last stake he sold was his portion of ownership of the Astros ballclub. He was indicted into the Texas Baseball Hall of Fame in 2006, the Astros Hall of Fame in 2021, and the Texas Sports Hall of Fame in 2024. Hofheinz died on November 22, 1982, at age seventy.

General Manager
Harold B. "Spec" Richardson

Spec Richardson began his career managing concessions in his hometown of Columbus, Georgia, for the minor league teams there before joining the Houston franchise as the business manager. He was promoted to full-time general manager in 1967. In addition to the trades that released Sonny Jackson, Dave Giusti, Bob Aspromonte, Mike Cuellar, and Rusty Staub from the Astros, Spec Richardson dealt away Orange Crush Astros members Joe Morgan, Cesar Geronimo, and Jack Billingham, along with Denis Menke and Ed Armbrister, to the Cincinnati Reds following the 1971 season. This trade is often considered the most lopsided in MLB history and therefore Richardson's worst. He later traded Jimmy Wynn and Lee May, the latter being acquired in the trade with the Reds, before he was fired in 1975 and replaced by Tal Smith. From 1975 to 1981, he served as general manager for the San Francisco Giants, where he orchestrated a trade for Vida Blue in 1978. Richardson died on April 12, 2016, at age ninety-three.

Vice President, Director of Player Personnel
Tal Smith

Tal Smith came to Houston from the Cincinnati Reds' front office in late 1960, and when the Colt 45s began play in 1962, he was the Farm System Director. During construction of the Astrodome, Smith was the primary advisor over ensuring that the structure, and later the artificial grass surface, was suitable for Major League play. After the firing of general manager Paul Richards in 1965, Smith was given the title of Vice President and Director of Player Personnel, which he held until the New York Yankees hired Smith in 1973. He returned to Houston in 1975 to take the general manager position, and he built up the eventual 1980 National League Western Division Champion Astros roster. Smith was controversially fired after the season, so he founded his own team consulting firm to help ballclubs handle arbitration called *Tal Smith Enterprises*. He rejoined the Astros' front office from 1994 to 2011, and during that stretch he advised with the construction of Enron Field (Now Daikin Park), so a 30-degree hill in center field was created and named Tal's Hill in Smith's honor. The hill remained until its removal in 2016. He was awarded with Baseball America's Lifetime Achievement Award in 2005 and inducted into the Astros Hall of Fame in 2022.

Orange Crush That Got Away
35 Mike Cuellar, 20-9, 3.08 ERA for Baltimore in 1971

Mike Cuellar pitched for the Baltimore Orioles until 1976, and his Major League career was over after a cup of coffee with the California Angels in 1977, though he still pitched in the Mexican League until 1983. He served as a pitching instructor in Puerto Rico and Baltimore until he died on April 2, 2010, at age seventy-two.

39 Dave Giusti, 5-6, 2.93 ERA, 30 saves for Pittsburgh in 1971

After winning the World Series with the Pittsburgh Pirates in 1971, Dave Giusti made the All Star team in 1973. Four years later, he was with the Oakland A's and Chicago Cubs, but he soon retired in 1977. He later became a corporate sales manager for American Express.

53 Mike Marshall, 5-8, 4.28 ERA, 23 saves for Montreal in 1971

Mike Marshall came up through the Philadelphia Phillies' and Detroit Tigers' organizations and made his MLB debut in the Motor City in 1967, and was later a member of the one-season Seattle Pilots expansion ballclub in 1969. He was rejected by the Tigers, Pilots, and Astros because of the same reason: they did not like him throwing a screwball. However, Marshall continued throwing the pitch when he ended up with the Montreal Expos in June 1970 because he determined that it was safer than other breaking balls. This physiological pitching knowledge would become a trademark of Marshall's and would come to benefit him as he settled into the role of relief pitcher, becoming the first to ever win the Cy Young Award in 1974, as a member of the Los Angeles Dodgers. He had stints with the Atlanta Braves, Texas Rangers, Minnesota Twins, and New York Mets, then hung up the spikes in 1983 while at the Triple-A level, though he did continue pitching in sandlot leagues until the age of 56. He continued trying to teach his modern pitching mechanics and expertise, but very few people were interested. Marshall died on May 31, 2021, at age seventy-eight.

8 Jerry Grote, .270, 2 HR, 35 RBI for New York Mets in 1971

Jerry Grote led all catchers in the National League in putouts and range factor in 1971. Injuries began to hit Grote in the mid-70's and in 1977 he was traded to the Los Angeles Dodgers. He played a full season before retiring, though the Kansas City Royals successfully talked Grote into coming back for the 1981 season. He attempted a meat-selling business before coaching in the Detroit Tigers' organization. Grote has been inducted into four Halls of Fame: the Texas Baseball Hall of Fame, New York Mets Hall of Fame, San Antonio Sports Hall of Fame, and the Trinity University Athletic Hall of Fame. He broadcasted Round Rock Express games in 2010 and 2011. Grote died on April 7, 2024, at age eighty-one.

25 Nate Colbert, .264, 27, 84 RBI for Padres in 1971

Nate Colbert was selected by the new San Diego Padres in the 1968 Expansion Draft, where he made a name for himself as the Padres' first big league star. He made the All Star team in 1971 and 1973. Injuries began to plague Colbert in 1974, and he was traded to the Detroit Tigers after the season. Midway through 1975, he was sold to the Montreal Expos and made his last MLB appearance with the Oakland A's in late-1976 before retiring due to his back issues. Colbert was the Padres' franchise home run leader until 2024 and remained in the organization's good graces when he coached in the organization's minor league system. Later in life, he became an ordained minister. Colbert died on January 5, 2023, at age seventy-six.

11 Sandy Alomar, .260, 4 HR, 42 RBI for Angels in 1971

Sandy Alomar spent his playing career with the Milwaukee/Atlanta Braves, New York Mets, Chicago White Sox, California Angels, New York Yankees, and Texas Rangers, and spanned a coaching career beginning in 1986 with the San Diego Padres, Chicago Cubs, Colorado Rockies, and Mets, retiring from coaching in 2009. He made the American League All Star team while with the Angels in 1970. His oldest son, Sandy Alomar Jr., played for 20 seasons and has coached for the Mets and Cleveland Indians/Guardians, filling in as manager for the latter in 2012 and is still currently a coach in Cleveland. His youngest son is Hall of Famer Roberto Alomar.

14 Bob Aspromonte, .225, 5 HR, 33 RBI for Mets in 1971

Bob Aspromonte finished his career with the New York Mets in 1971. He has been inducted in several Halls of Fame: the Texas Baseball Hall of Fame, National Italian American Sports Hall of Fame, and the Astros Hall of Fame. Aspromonte retired to Houston and became a businessman after he retired from playing. He is the younger brother of former Major League manager Ken Aspromonte.

16 Sonny Jackson, .258, 2 HR, 25 RBI for Braves in 1971

Sonny Jackson played for the Atlanta Braves until 1974, the same team he returned to coach for in 1982 and 1983. He resumed coaching in 1997 and retired in 2006, spending time with the San Francisco Giants and Chicago Cubs during those years.

15 Manny Mota, .312, 0 HR, 34 RBI for Dodgers in 1971

Manny Mota played for the San Francisco Giants, Pittsburgh Pirates, Montreal Expos, and Los Angeles Dodgers. He made the National League All Star team in 1973 and won two World Series in 1981 and 1988, all with the Dodgers. He remained with the Dodgers after his last playing season of 1988 as a coach, and he moved to the Spanish broadcast booth in 2013. Mota has been inducted into the Caribbean Baseball Hall of Fame (1998), Hispanic Heritage Baseball Museum Hall of Fame (2003), and Baseball Reliquary's Baseball Shrine of the Eternals in 2013. He has two sons, Andy and Jose, who also played Major League ball.

10 Rusty Staub, .311, 19 HR, 97 RBI for Expos in 1971

Rusty Staub was the first bona fide star in Montreal Expos history until he was traded to the New York Mets for the 1972 season. He later spent time with the Detroit Tigers and Texas Rangers, with second stints with Montreal and New York falling between those. Staub made six All Star teams, had his number 10 retired by the Montreal Expos in 1993, and was inducted into the New York Mets Hall of Fame in 1986. Staub worked in and operated several charity organizations until he died on March 28, 2018, at age seventy-three.

Manager
1 Grady Hatton

Grady Hatton remained with the Astros after his firing as manager, first as a scout from 1968 to 1972, and then as a big league coach in 1973 and 1974, as well as director of player development in 1975. He continued scouting for the San Francisco Giants into the late 1980's. He was inducted into the Texas Baseball Hall of Fame in 1996 along with Roger Metzger and George W. Bush. Hatton died on April 11, 2013, at age ninety.

Manager
26 Luman Harris

Shortly after his firing from the Astros, Lum Harris followed Paul Richards to Atlanta and became the manager of the triple-A Richmond Braves in 1967. He was granted the big league job for the 1969 campaign and led the team to the NL West championship, the only time Harris would ever finish in first place in his Major League Baseball life. After being fired during the 1972 season, he returned to his Birmingham farm and vowed to never leave until he died. He kept that promise and died on November 11, 1996, at age eighty-one.

Hitting/First Base Coach
3 Mel McGaha

Mel McGaha played in the St. Louis Cardinals organization but achieved greater success managing clubs such as the Shreveport Sports, Mobile Bears, Toronto Maple Leafs, and Oklahoma City 89ers. He coached and briefly managed with the Cleveland Indians and Kansas City A's before coming to the Astros' organization. McGaha also had a career in basketball, playing one season for the New York Knicks and coaching for two seasons at what was then called Arkansas A&M College. As a member of the 1948 minor league Duluth Dukes, he survived a July 24 bus crash that killed their manager and four players. McGaha died on February 2, 2002, at age seventy-five.

Principle Owner
R. E. "Bob" Smith

Bob Smith joined George Kirksey, Craig Cullinan, and Roy Hofheinz in the Houston Sports Association to bring Major League Baseball to Houston. Prior to this, he made his wealth as an oil tycoon, as Cullinan's grandfather had by founding Texaco. After his baseball endeavors, he spent a lot of time on his ranches throughout Harris County where he raised cattle. Smith died on November 29, 1973, at age seventy-nine.

General Manager

Paul Richards

Paul Richards played as a catcher from 1932 to 1946 for the Brooklyn Dodgers, New York Giants, Philadelphia Athletics, and Detroit Tigers, whom he won a World Series with in 1945. He then became a manager from 1951 to 1961 for the Chicago White Sox and Baltimore Orioles, as well as an additional season with the White Sox in 1976. He served as the Orioles' general manager from 1955 to 1958, and he arrived in Houston after he finished managing the Orioles. After his firing from the Astros, Richards took the same job with the Atlanta Braves, whom he helped to the 1969 National League West division title. During his managerial career, he pioneered moving a pitcher to the outfield temporarily during a game and bringing another one in to pitch in order to keep the original pitcher in the game so he could pitch later. This move became known as the "Waxahachie Swap" after Richards' nickname of the "Waxahachie Wizard," since he was from Waxahachie, Texas, where he was born and where he died on May 4, 1986, at age seventy-seven.

The Astrodome

The Eighth Wonder of the World

Before the 1968 MLB All Star Game took place inside the Astrodome, Astros broadcaster Gene Elston gave NBC viewers a detailed tour around the Dome, describing the playing field and its dimensions, as well as its luxuries:

"The fabulous Astrodome, the Eighth Wonder of the World. So let's see what the place looks like:

For the first time in history, the All Star Game will be played in air-conditioned comfort under a dome high enough to place a twelve-story building

(Some sources reported that the Dome could actually fit an eighteen-story building inside).

Being a perfectly symmetrical ballpark, there are few problems involved when it comes to the batted ball. Fences are 340' down each foul line, 390' to right and left-center field, and 406' to center (By 1971, the distance to the alleys were down from 390' to 375'). *Now you'll note the yellow lines and the fences. Any ball hitting this line or above is a home run. Now the dugouts here in the Astrodome are the longest in baseball: 120 feet which also includes the bullpen pitchers and catchers.*

Spectators walk down eighty percent of the stadium seats, more than any other stadium. The seating capacity here is forty-five thousand for baseball. All seats are theatre-type cushioned chairs, color-coded to match the spectators' ticket. Seating is on six levels, with the field seats mechanically movable for football seating. Five restaurants, two private clubs for baseball stadiums, and more than tomorrow, it's modern.

And as if that's not enough, let's take a look into the far-reaches of the ninth level here at the Astrodome. Now, don't think by the pictures that we're leaving baseball and the Astrodome—on the contrary. This is a look into one of the over fifty luxurious skyboxes on the ninth level. Boxes containing twenty-four to thirty seats adjacent to the clubrooms. Each clubroom is individually designed with a different motif. Magnificently furnished and containing all the comforts, as you can see, telephone, radio, television, even closed-circuit TVs for viewing the ballgame that's in progress and will be here tonight. Restrooms, icemaker and bar, and of course, special elevators take the skybox holders to their very special clubrooms.

You know, many adjectives have been used to describe the Astrodome, but somehow, they all seem inadequate. You know, it is generally agreed that no one man could have built the Astrodome. But, without Judge Roy Hofheinz, owner and president of the Houston Sports Association and the Houston Astros, it would certainly not be a reality today. Now just completed this year in the right field outfield area are Judge Hofheinz's private quarters. From the ninth-level Polynesian bar down through five additional levels, you'll find almost a complete city. The Presidential suite, plus four other suites with facilities for sleeping over fourteen people. Beauty parlor, barber shop, children's play area, small movie theatre, a boardroom where the National and the American Leagues will hold their meetings tomorrow, and of course, a complete recreation area.

From the gondola, 208 feet overhead, you get this unique view of the Astrodome"

This definitely is the Astrodome, and this is baseball tomorrow-style. Modern baseball inside, in air-conditioned comfort. You know, one gentleman once said 'You have to see it, to believe it, and somehow, even then you don't.' And we certainly hope, that you fans, wherever you may be, will have an opportunity to get to Houston, and see the fabulous, Eighth Wonder, of the World.[1]

Elston was the primary Astros radio broadcaster, and fans in attendance also had a unique voice in that of public address announcer J. Fred Duckett, who gained notoriety when Jose Cruz joined the team in 1975 and would verbally elongate the outfielder's last name as "Cruuuuuuuuuz," to much fanfare.

Most Dome games started at 7:30 p.m. local time, and Sunday afternoon games began at 2:00 p.m., with two exceptions: May 2 against the Mets began at 3:00 p.m., and July 18 against the Phillies began at 1:30 p.m. because it was a doubleheader.

The field box seats (Sections 100) were colored in red, the pavilion outfield seats (Sections 200) were orange, the club level seats (Sections 300) were black, the loge level seats (Sections 400) were purple, the upper level seats (Sections 500) were yellow, and the Sky Box seats were blue. Pavilion and general admission seating was only sold on the day of the game unless all other tickets were sold out.

The Astrodome ticket office was open daily from 9 a.m. to 5 p.m. Tickets could also be purchased from Foley's Department Stores in Houston, Houston Citizens Bank and Trust at Main and Jefferson, and Montgomery Ward stores around the Southwest US. By mail, fans could send a check or money order to Tickets, Houston Astros, P.O. Box 1691 in Houston. Game date, type of tickets, number of tickets, and 25 cents for shipping and handling were required to process a mail ticket order.

Box seat tickets were $4.00, Reserved seat tickets were $3.00, and General Admission seat tickets were $1.50. Sundays at the Dome were "Family Day," and children under 14 received a $1 off any ticket. The same applied to Wednesdays, which were Ladies Nights, so ladies received the same discount. One of many parts of Judge Hofheinz's genius when designing the Dome was using colors of seats and lights that would best accentuate women's clothes and makeup so every game would be Ladies' Night.[2]

The Astrodome had a capacity of 47,000, and the highest-attended home game, July 17, was attended by 32,852 fans. 1971 was the seventh consecutive season that the Astros drew over one million fans, partly due to sustained interest in seeing the Astrodome. Per game, the Astros attracted 15,575 on average, which was ninth in the National League and eleventh in Major League Baseball, putting Houston in the lower percentile for average fans per game in the league but in the upper percentile in all of baseball.

The outfield wall was 17 feet, 11 inches tall both from the left field foul line to left/center where the pavilion section started and from right/center where the pavilion section ended to the right field foul line. Between those, the fence measured 13 feet, 10 inches.

AstroTurf was produced by Monsanto under the name ChemGrass, but Hofheinz coined the term AstroTurf for the Dome's surface. The grounds crew, referred to as "Earthmen," wore orange spaceman's suits and, along with dragging the infield dirt to smooth it out, used brooms to sweep dirt off the artificial turf back onto the dirt, and even vacuumed the surface at times. The artificial grass did have negative effects such as being harder if fallen on and causing batted balls to roll and skip a lot quicker, so slower infielders struggled, sometimes having to move to the outfield. However, the positives of AstroTurf benefit a quick, defensively gifted, and pitching-heavy ballclub…like the Astros. Players like Sonny Jackson and Joe Morgan could simply beat the ball into the ground, and it would bounce high into the air, or else roll too fast for opposing infielders who were used to natural grass to handle, and easily reach first base with a hit. This would set up a deep, multi-dimensional heart of the order to bring them in to score. Cesar Cedeno and Jimmy Wynn both also had great speed and ability to hit for contact, and they complimented that with power and slugging ability, which the following batters of Rusty Staub, Bob Watson, Doug Rader, and Jerry Grote had at the expense of speed.

Houston pitchers, catchers, and infielders often wore shoes with metal spikes on the bottom since they were on dirt when hitting, running, and playing defensively. Some outfielders, on the other hand, often used shoes with molded traction on the bottom that would be less likely to rip up the Turf. These are just general rules, however; each individual player might use rubber cleats one day and metal spikes the next, depending on what position they are playing, whether they are starting or not, what shoes they wore the previous day, the importance of the game, or whatever else may have come to their mind. Rusty Staub, for instance, found a pair of soccer cleats with molded traction on the bottom to wear while in the outfield or running the bases. When he batted, he wore one traditional steel-spiked baseball shoe and one soccer shoe, and if he reached base, he would swap the baseball shoe or the other soccer one.[3]

Right fielder Rusty Staub uniquely carried two pairs of shoes – metal spiked, and rubber spiked – for use on grass and turf and on AstroTurf, respectively.

Whitey Diskin was the Astros' clubhouse manager, and Jim "Doc" Ewell was the athletic trainer. The ballclub's traveling secretary was Art Perkins.

The visitors' dugout was on the third base side, and the Astros' dugout was on the first base side. Just as both dugouts were longer than those of other ballparks, both clubhouses were expansive by comparison to other ballparks such as Wrigley Field in Chicago, though teams like the Cincinnati Reds, Pittsburgh Pirates, and Philadelphia Phillies had by now left their respective quaint, baseball shrines of Crosley Field, Forbes Field, and Shibe Park/Connie Mack Stadium, and moved to their own round, concrete stadiums of Riverfront Stadium, Three Rivers Stadium, and Veterans Stadium.

Concessions were priced as follows:
15 cents: 7 oz. Soda, 6 oz. Coffee
25 cents: 12 oz. Soda, 10 oz. Coffee, Potato Chips, Peanuts, Popcorn Megaphone
35 cents: Hot Dog
40 cents: Pizza Roll, Corn Dog
45 cents: Chili Dog
55 cents: Draft Beer, Bottled Beer
65 cents: Foot Long Hot Dog, Hamburger
80 cents: Texas Size Beer
85 cents: Chick-Fil-A
95 cents: Corn Beef Sandwich, Ham Sandwich, Roast Beef Sandwich
$1.10: Roast Beef Sandwich with Cheese

Team stores and merchandise/souvenir shops were open as Gift Shops behind first base on the mezzanine level and behind home plate on the field box level, and as Satellite Shops throughout the Astrodome. Galaxie Gifts was another popular name for souvenir stands and stores in the Dome, and the Astros' current triple-A affiliate, the Sugar Land Space Cowboys, use the name for their team shop. Merchandise was priced as follows:

Autographed Baseball: $4.50
Astros Baseball: 50 cents and $2.00
Mini Wood Bat: 75 cents
Baseball Bank: $1.50
Bat Rack Bank: $2.00
Cap: $1.50, $2.00, and $2.50
Charms: $1.50, $2.50, and $5.00

Plastic Coasters: $1.50
Metal Coasters: $1.50 individual, $7.95 for set of eight
Doll Spacette: $3.50 and $5.00
Field Folding Glasses: $2.75
Astros Helmet: $2.00
Baseball Holder: $2.00
Nylon Astros Jacket: $5.00, $5.50, and $6.25
Key Chain: $1.50 and $2.00
Lighter: $4.00
Money Clip: $2.00
Necklace: $2.50
Pajamas: $3.00
Pencil: 10 cents and 50 cents
Ballpoint Pen: $1.00
Pennant: $1.00
Salt and Pepper Shakers: $2.00
Plastic Shopping Bag: 25 cents
Sweatshirt: $4.00
Tie Bar: $2.00
T-Shirt: $2.00
Thermos Set of Six: $7.95
Ashtray: $3.00
Uniform: $8.50
Glass Mug: $1.00 and $1.50

Program/Scorecard: 35 cents, cover featuring a basic color background with player pictured in action along with their printed signature, the matchup near the top, and the Astrodome near the bottom.

Red: vs Braves, Johnny Edwards on cover
    vs Mets, Jack Billingham
    vs Twins, Norm Miller
Bright Orange: vs Giants, Fred Gladding

vs Cardinals, Denis Menke
vs Padres, Doug Rader (Batting)
vs N/A, Joe Morgan
Dark Orange: vs Phillies, Jack Hiatt
vs Padres, Cesar Cedeno
vs Cardinals, Roger Metzger (Batting)
vs Yankees and Twins, Denny Lemaster
Yellow: vs Mets, Ken Forsch
vs Giants, Denis Menke
vs Cubs, Roger Metzger (Fielding)
vs N/A, Joe Morgan
Gold: vs Pirates, Don Wilson x2
vs Expos, Bob Watson
Green: vs Dodgers, Doug Rader (Fielding)
vs Expos, Wade Blasingame
vs Giants, Larry Dierker
vs Reds, Jesus Alou
Royal Blue: vs Cubs, George Culver
vs Braves, Jim Ray
vs Phillies, Marty Martinez
vs Dodgers, Cesar Geronimo
vs Reds, Fred Gladding
vs Yankees, Denny Lemaster
Light Blue: vs Reds, Jimmy Wynn

The stores had merchandise and souvenirs for both the Astros baseball team and the Astrodome, since the Dome itself was considered a tourist attraction. Tours of the ballpark were available at 11 a.m., 1 p.m., and 3 p.m., with a 5 p.m. time slot added from June 1 through Labor Day. If there was an afternoon event, the only tour was scheduled for 10 a.m. Tours were $1.00 per person, children under six were admitted free, and lasted about an hour. Large groups of at least fifty people could call and make special arrangements.

The remainder of the AstroDomain consisted of the AstroHall convention center, AstroWorld amusement park, and AstroWorld Hotel. AstroWorld closed in 2005 and was demolished soon after, and the Astro-Hall has been replaced by NRG Arena and NRG Center, leaving only the Dome and the Hotel standing from the original empire. The Hotel is now under Wyndham ownership and operates under the name Wyndham Houston Near NRG Park/Medical Center. On the top level still sits Hofheinz's suite he had built there, with a two-story living area resembling the Astrodome interior, complete with a scale-replica scoreboard that copied, in real time, the numbers, letters, and spectacles that the Astrolite scoreboard just across the street in the Dome displayed.

The expansive AstroDomain consisted of the prominent Astrodome, which was later joined by the AstroHall convention center, the AstroWorld amusement park, the AstroWorld Hotel, and even an AstroTram to navigate the estate.

No description of the Astrodome would be complete without mention of the AstroLite. Operated by publicity director Wayne Chandler, the scoreboard was considered the signature that made the Dome stand out among other mutli-purpose ballparks as more teams indulged in roofs and turf, and it gave Houston and the National League a taste of what Bill Veeck had conjured up at Comiskey Park in Chicago for the White Sox. The first-of-its-kind $2 million scoreboard in the outfield was four stories tall, 474 feet long across center field, 300 tons, over half an acre in square units, and used 1200 miles of wiring and 50,000 lights to project Texas-appropriate animations.[4] The show began once an Astro was declared to have hit a home run or once the Astros had finished off a win. The Astrodome would show up on the left side of the scoreboard and a rocket would shoot out of it, flying toward the right side where it would explode into a baseball or fireball with the words "Home Run!" inside of it (When celebrating a win, the animations up to this point were omitted). Those words would blink four times, then the Dome and fireball would be replaced by two cowboys with pistols that aimed up and down and fired in sync with each other as the bullets bounced off the edges of the scoreboard in red, white, and blue. Those cowboys then faded out and two bulls with an American flag on one horn and a Texas flag on another, came into focus, blowing dust out of their noses, then to round it out, a cowboy on a horse is shown chasing a bull and successfully lassoing it… all of this with appropriate sound effects echoing throughout the stadium.

Obviously, the Astros were amazed by the electronic show the scoreboard put on when the staff played it before the team's first practice there, so their hitters were motivated to muscle home runs to warrant the scoreboard spectacle and the entire team wanted to win so it would play after the game. As for the visitors, they knew anytime it was played meant bad news for them, but the show was not simply an indication of something not going their way. This was during a more conservative time in society, and in baseball, which was seen as a gentleman's game, common practice

The Eighth Wonder of the World was the pride of the Space City for many years, and Astros players took pride in calling it home.

after a home run was to simply hit the ball, run until the ball flies over the fence, keep up a light jog, and step on home plate in stride as you head back to the dugout, all while the organist might play a special tune to celebrate, but that would be about it. This interruption of that unwritten respect angered opposing pitchers, who not only had just given up a home run, but now had to watch and hear this scoreboard celebration for 40-45 seconds, longer than it took for the batter to circle the bases and reach the dugout. The Braves (Then still in Milwaukee) combated the Astros on this in July 1965 by smuggling their own fireworks on their road trip that took them through Houston, so after they finished their series in San Francisco and Los Angeles, they arrived at the Astrodome in Houston on the 26th, waited for one of them to go deep, which catcher Joe Torre did off Larry Dierker, then they let 'em rip, firing off firecrackers and sparklers. The fans enjoyed the creativity. However, in all other cases, if the AstroLite was given the chance to show off enough, it could quite possibly open the floodgates for the now-motivated Astros as they tee off on a frustrated pitcher, who only becomes more so as he continues to struggle, all because of revolutionary technology that would today seem archaic.

Many people have been quoted with their thoughts about the Eighth Wonder of the World:

Larry Dierker: *"I feel like I've just walked into the next century."*

"When we came back from Spring Training in 1965, we all knew that we were going to the Astrodome, not Colt Stadium. Everyone was really eager with anticipation. And I remember as we came into the Dome parking lot, the lights were on inside. We were so excited, we went right out onto the field. Believe me, it was breathtaking. The colors were amazing; every level was a different color. The scoreboard was so gigantic; nobody had ever seen anything like that. Being from Los Angeles, I'd been to Dodger Stadium a few times; it was considered the best stadium in the National League. Well the Astrodome made Dodger Stadium look old-fashioned."[5]

Norm Miller: *"This can't be a ballpark. It looked like it had just landed from outer space. Jaws dropped, eyes bulged—our first encounter with the unknown. Enormous! Imagine indoor baseball. Yes, it had an infield, and fences way out there. But my god, a roof? Nobody was moving or saying anything definitive. Just oohs and aahs. Frozen in our disbelief; this was the new home of baseball and it belonged to the Houston Astros."*[6]

"Every time I walked into the Dome I was amazed. Sometimes during a game, I would look up at that roof in disbelief we were actually playing indoors, and when the storms came we just kept on playing."[7]

Doug Rader: *"It was unbelievable to walk into the dome. I had been in there before, after the 1965 season they had a few of us come in and work out while the club was there. Being on the field with that many people there was thrilling. I was floating on air."*[8]

Grady Hatton: *"This is the real utopia for baseball—no wind, no sun, no rain, no bad bounces."*[9]

Mickey Herskowitz, Houston Post writer: *"The Astrodome looks like a giant underarm deodorant bottle that's been buried, standing up, with only its neck and roller head top now visible above the ground!"*[10]

Paul Pryor, National League Umpire: *"The Astrodome was a big, beautiful new park with luxurious seats, controlled temperatures and an umpires' dressing room that was as big as a modest water closet when it was built. Shortly after the ribbon-cutting ceremonies, the Astrodome's management acceded to the umpires' demands that their locker room be built a little more spacious. Walls were knocked down and a new dressing room was equipped with chairs, a couch, a refrigerator and a color television."*[11]

1971 National League Umpire Roster

The umpires that the National League employed and that graced the AstroTurf in 1971:

1-Al Barlick
2-Ken Burkhart
3-Nick Colosi
4-Shag Crawford
5-Dave "Satch" Davidson
6-Jerry Dale
7-Augie Donatelli
8-Bob Engel
9-Tom Gorman
10-Doug Harvey
11-John Kibler
12-Stan Landes
13-Andy Olsen
14-Chris Pelekoudas
15-Paul Pryor
16-Bruce Froemming
17-Mel Steiner
18-Dick Stello
19-Ed Sudol
20-Ed Vargo
21-Tony Venzon
22-Harry Wendlestedt
23-Lee Weyer
24-Bill Williams

Hotels Away from Home
The hotels the Astros stayed in when on the road in 1971:

Atlanta: Marriott
Chicago: Executive House
Cincinnati: Netherland Hilton
Los Angeles: Biltmore
Montreal: Queen Elizabeth
New York: Roosevelt
Philadelphia: Bellevue-Stratford
Pittsburgh: William Penn
St. Louis: Chase Park Plaza
San Diego: El Cortez
San Francisco: Sheraton Place

Minor Leagues
The Astros' affiliates in the minor leagues in 1971:

Triple-A: Oklahoma City 89ers, American Association
Double-A: Columbus (GA) Astros (Southern League, of the Dixie Association)
Single-A: Cocoa Astros (Florida State League)
Sumter Astros (Western Carolinas League)
Rookie: Covington (VA) Astros (Appalachian League)

CITATIONS

Introduction

1   Morgan, Joe, and David Falkner. Joe Morgan: A Life in Baseball. W.W. Norton & Co., 1993. (Pg. 102)

Background

1   Brown, Bill, and Mike Acosta. Houston Astros: Deep in the Heart: Blazing a Trail From Expansion to World Series. Bright Sky Press, 2013.

2   Pratt, Joseph and Dierker, Larry, Houston Public Library Digital Archives, 14 July 2008, cdm17006.contentdm.oclc.org/digital/collection/p17006coll126/id/68/rec/2. Accessed 18 Nov. 2023.

3   Morgan. (Pg. 66)

4   Nowlin, Bill, and Wood, Brian. "Grady Hatton." Society for American Baseball Research, 9 Apr. 2020, sabr.org/bioproj/person/grady-hatton/.

5   "Minor League Baseball Statistics and Rosters on Statscrew.Com." Stats Crew, www.statscrew.com/minorbaseball/roster/.

6   Vance, Mike, and Samuel Barrett.

7   Baseball-Reference. www.baseball-reference.com/.

8   Wynn, Jimmy, and Bill McCurdy. *Toy Cannon: The Autobiography of Baseball's Jimmy Wynn.* McFarland & Co., 2010. (Pg. 74-75)

9   Sports Illustrated, 6 June 1966. (Cover)

10   Smith, Tal, and Samuel Barrett. "Phone Call W/ Tal Smith, #2." 15 July 2024.

11 "1967 MLB All-Star Game Highlights." YouTube, Big W's Sports Memories, 23 July 2019, youtu.be/4VgIDkzDqVY?si=RvusqwlJD-vNHE21f. Accessed 11 May 2024.

12 Wynn. (Pg. 87)

13 "HOU@CIN: Wynn's Tape-Measure Shot at Crosley Field." YouTube, MLB, 10 June 2013, youtu.be/EQ2f-s9p-J3s?si=uZSw-gBG_LyqSI7x.

14 "Wynn Hits Tape-Measure Blast at Forbes Field." YouTube, MLB, 12 Feb. 2015, youtu.be/Y4Cn6qusV3c?si=yoWb7a181AXcNNOS. Accessed 11 May 2024.

15 Watson, Bob, and Russ Pate. Survive To Win. Thomas Nelson Publishers, 1997. (Pg. 94)

16 Florio, John, and Ouisie Shapiro. "When King Died, Major League Baseball Struck Out." Andscape, 4 Apr. 2018, andscape.com/features/when-martin-luther-king-died-major-league-baseball-struck-out/.

17 Morgan. (Pg. 67-69)

18 Riis, Richard. "April 15, 1968: The Astrodome Marathon: Astros Beat Mets 1-0 in 24-Inning Duel." Society for American Baseball Research, 17 Apr. 2020, sabr.org/gamesproj/game/april-15-1968-the-astrodome-marathon-astros-beat-mets-1-0-in-24-inning-duel/. Accessed 19 Dec. 2024.

19 Miller, Norm. *To All My Fans...from Norm Who?* Double Play Productions, 2009. (Pg. i)

20 Wynn. (Pg. 95)

21 Wynn. (Pg. 97)

22 Wynn. (Pg. 96)

23 Astros Daily. Astrosdaily.com

24 Wynn. (Pg. 99-103)

25 Centerfieldmaz@gmail.com, Contact @. "Remembering Mets History: (1968) Mets & Astros Brawl at the Houston Astrodome." Centerfield Maz, Blogger, 15 Jan. 2023, www.centerfieldmaz.com/2020/08/remembering-mets-history-1968-mets.html.

26   Dierker, Larry. *This Ain't Brain Surgery: How to Win The Pennant Without Losing Your Mind.* Simon and Schuster, 2003. (Pg. 100)

27   Bouton, Jim. *Ball Four: The Final Pitch.* Original Edited in 1970 by Leonard Shecter, Turner, 2014. (Pg. 383)

28   Wilson, John. "Don Wilson Hurls 2nd No-Hitter of Career." AstrosDaily.com, www.astrosdaily.com/history/19690501/index.html. Accessed 02 Jan. 2025.

29   Wynn. (Pg. 116)

30   Bouton. (Pg. 325)

31   MLB.

32   Bouton. (Pg. 394)

33   Watson. (Pg. 106)

34   Astros Daily.

35   Vance, Mike, and Samuel Barrett. "Phone Call W/ Mike Vance." 4 Jan. 2024.

36   Baseball-Reference.

37   Dierker, Larry. *This Ain't Brain Surgery: How to Win The Pennant Without Losing Your Mind.* (Pg. 57-58)

March

1   Watson. (Pg. 84)

2   "Astros Figure To Have Best Shot Ever at Crown." Naugatuck Daily News, 1 Apr. 1971, p. 8.

3   "What Hofer Re-Signed with Astros in '71? - This Forgotten Day in Houston." YouTube, Houston Chronicle, 4 Mar. 2015, www.youtube.com/watch?v=ojQiW6XcYeI. Accessed 22 Mar. 2024.

4   Heiling, Joe. "Houston Holdout Morgan Seeking 'The Big Bundle.'" The Orlando Sentinel, 2 Mar. 1971, p. 39.

5   United Press International. "Money, Money, Money Spread Around Diamonds." The Times Herald, 3 Mar. 1971, p. 21.

6   "Joe Morgan Ends Astros Holdout, Signs." The Orlando Sentinel, 5 Mar. 1971, p. 37.

7   "What Hofer Re-Signed with Astros in '71? - This Forgotten Day in Houston."

8   "Papi's Pavilion Or Wise Gardens." The Orlando Sentinel, 12 June 1971, p. 5.

9   "9th Inning Astro Rally Snipped, Sox Win 4-3." The Orlando Sentinel, 6 Mar. 1971, p. 2.

10   "Astros Think Roger Metzger May Put Team In Contention." The Sacramento Bee, 6 Mar. 1971, p. 18.

11   "Astros Beat Kansas City." Del Rio News Herald, 7 Mar. 1971, p. 7.

12   "Spring Schedule." The Orlando Sentinel, 7 Mar. 1971, p. 61.

13   Wynn. (Pg. 129-130)

14   Wynn. (Pg. 126)

15   Rathet, Mike. "Astros Star-Bound?" The Billings Gazette, 24 Mar. 1971, p. 27.

16   "Geronimo Making Moves For Astros." San Angelo Standard-Times, 10 Mar. 1971, p. 15.

17   "Astros Boast Top Backstop Talent." The Waco Citizen, 11 Mar. 1971, p. 6.

18   Culver, George. The Earl of Oildale "Why Me?" 2024. (Pg. 78)

19   Smith, Tal, and Samuel Barrett. "Phone Call W/ Tal Smith, #1." 7 Mar. 2024.

20   Miller. (Pg. 154)

21   Spinks, Scipio, and Samuel Barrett. "Phone Call W/ Scipio Spinks." 7 Feb. 2025.

April

1   Verrell, Gordon. "Astros Outtasight -- Dodgers Second." Independent, 4 Apr. 1971, p. 77.

2   Morrison, Ronnie. "Lots Of Fun In Astrodome." Longview News-Journal, 6 Apr. 1971, p. 13.

3   "1971 - Dome Fans Are Treated to a 15-Inning Exhibition 'Tripleheader' between the Astros, Yankees and Twins. Houston Nips New York, 2-1, in the First Five-Inning Game and Later Tops

Minnesota, 5-3, in the Finale. in between, the Twins down the Yankees, 4-1." This Day In Baseball, Astros Daily, 2 Apr. 2021, thisdayinbaseball.com/1971-dome-fans-are-treated-to-a-15-inning-exhibition-tripleheader-between-the-astros-yankees-and-twins-houston-nips-new-york-2-1-in-the-first-five-inning-game-and-later-tops-minnesota-5/.

4   "Astros Host Unique Game In Astrodome." The Daily Plainsman, 4 Apr. 1971.

5   "YANKEES BEATEN BY ASTROS, 9 TO 3." The New York Times, 1 Apr. 1971.

6   "Astros Win Home Debut." The Brazosport Facts, 1 Apr. 1971, p. 6.

7   "Astros Seek Escape From April Doldrums." Abilene Reporter-News, 8 Mar. 1971, pp. 11-A.

8   Baseball-Reference.

9   Risinger, Bobby. "New Look, Fast Start." The Baytown Sun, 6 Apr. 1971, p. 6.

10 Lukas, Paul. "Uni Watch Glossary." Uni Watch, uni-watch.com/research-projects/uni-watchglossary/. Accessed 10 May 2024.

11 Barrett, Samuel. "Questions to Johnny Edwards." Received from Johnny Edwards, 16 Nov. 2022.

12 Lukas, Paul, and Jerry Reuss. "Uni Watch Profiles: Jerry Reuss, Part 2." Uni Watch, 17 Sept. 2010, uni-watch.com/2010/09/17/uni-watch-profiles-jerry-reuss-part-2/#google_vignette. Accessed 31 Jan. 2025.

13 Culver, George, and Samuel Barrett. "Phone Call W/ George Culver, Part 1." 25 Oct. 2024.

14 Morgan. (Pg. 113-114)

15 Bike, William S. Received by Samuel Barrett, Baseball Books, 18 Jan. 2024.

16 "Cubs Again Get 'Astro-Doomed.'" El Paso Herald-Post, 12 Apr. 1971, p. 18.

17 "Cubs 6 Astros 0." Lexington Herald-Leader, 10 Apr. 1971, p. 10.

18 "Astros Win, Wild Throw." The Sunday News, 11 Apr. 1971, p. 30.

19   "Astro-Graphs." Apr. 1971.

20   Spinks, Scipio, and Samuel Barrett.

21   "Astros Walk To 8-4 Win." Tampa Bay Times/St. Petersburg Times, 14 Apr. 1971, p. 33.

22   Holtz, Sean. "Norm Miller Home Runs." Baseball Almanac, www.baseball-almanac.com/players/home_run.php?p=milleno01. Accessed 20 May 2024.

23   Morgan. (Pg. 114)

24   "Astros Call Chiles." Fort Worth Star-Telegram, 20 Apr. 1971, p. 22.

25   "'Balk' Jenkins Wraps Up Astros." Belvidere Daily Republican, 21 Apr. 1971, p. 6.

26   "Dierker Fires Five-Hitter To Lead Astros Past Cubs." Victoria Advocate, 23 Apr. 1971, p. 16.

27   Nissenson, Herschel. "Mauch's Montreal, S'ilvous Plait, Sweeps Astros For First In NL East." The Daily Times-News, 26 Apr. 1971, p. 13.

28   "Dierker Proves Stopper As Astros Edge Phillies." The Miami Herald, 29 Apr. 1971, p. 185.

29   "Houston Fielder Tears Up Phils With His Stick." The Odessa American, 29 Apr. 1971, p. 9.

May

1   Benshoff, Al. "Astros Flatten Phillies 8-1." Intelligencer Journal, 8 May 1971, p. 13.

2   Demling, Tanner. "How Johns Hopkins and Navy Brought Lacrosse to Texas." Lacrosse Bucket, 23 Apr. 2020, lacrossebucket. com/2020/04/23/how-johns-hopkins-and-navy-brought-lacrosse-to-texas/. Accessed 29 Dec. 2024.

3   Firmite, Ron. "A GOOD ONE FOR THE BOOKS." Sports Illustrated, 24 May 1971.

4   Barrett, Samuel, and Larry Dierker. "Astros Conversation W/ Larry Dierker." 2 Apr. 2024.

5   Astros Daily. "1971 - Doug Rader Belts a Grand Slam and Drives in Six to Pace a 12-4 Thumping of the Cardinals. His Two-Run Double in the Third Follows the First-Inning Slam. Jack Hiatt and Roger Metzger Add Three Hits Apiece in the 17-Hit Performance." This Day In Baseball, 2 May 2023, thisdayinbaseball.com/1971-doug-rader-belts-a-grand-slam-and-drives-in-six-to-pace-a-12-4-thumping-of-the-cardinals-his-two-run-double-in-the-third-follows-the-first-inning-slam-jack-hiatt-and/. Accessed 10 June 2024.

6   "Hungry Astros Kick Cardinals." The Manhattan Mercury, 17 May 1971, p. 8.

7   "Astros Call Up Mayberry." Corpus Christi Times, 21 May 1971, p. 45.

8   "Cobbler's Best Friend Hurls Astros Over S.F." Daily Independent Journal, 22 May 1971, p. 23.

9   "Astro Rookie's Hit in 12th Beats Giants 2-1." The Honolulu Advertiser, 23 May 1971, p. 82.

10   Carnicelli, Joe. "Astros' Dierker Still Trying For No-Hitter." The Miami Herald, 28 May 1971, p. 40.

11   Carnicelli.

12   Carnicelli.

13   Barrett, Samuel, and Larry Dierker.

14   "Rained Out 89ers Await Astros." The Daily Oklahoman, 27 May 1971, p. 29.

15   Lawson, Earl. "Wilson, Dierker, et al... Not What Reds Need." The Cincinnati Post, 28 May 1971, p. 36.

16   Lawson, Earl. "Hal(p) Due For The Reds." The Cincinnati Post, 29 May 1971, p. 10.

17   "Reds Edge Astros, 2-1, On Error In Seventh." The Daily News, 31 May 1971, p. 192.

18   "Astros Backer Dies." News-Press, 1 June 1971, p. 14.

19   "Pitching Coach Predicts 25 Wins For Astro Hurler Dierker." The Daily Advocate, 1 June 1971, p. 13.

June

1   "Astros Still Hot - - Cedeno Is Thriving On Braves Pitching." The Baytown Sun, 2 June 1971, p. 16.
2   "Stargell Blasts Bucs By Astros." Tyler Morning Telegraph, 7 June 1971, p. 10.
3   Yake, Byron. "Virdon Steps Down As Buc Pilot." The Evening Standard, 7 June 1971, p. 17.
4   "Walker Likes Those Pirates Hitters...Bucs Outlast Harry's 'Hitless' Astros 9-8." Simpson's Leader-Times, 7 June 1971, p. 16.
5   "Cedeno Breaks Up Kelley's No-Hitter, But Astros Lose." The Kilgore News Herald, 11 June 1971, p. 2.
6   "Astros To Honor Doug Rader." Longview News-Journal, 7 June 1971, p. 12.
7   McMane, Fred. "Wild Pitch Difference As Giants Edge Mets." The Columbus Telegram, 12 June 1971, p. 6.
8   Miller. (Pg. 149)
9   "Astros 9, LA 7." The Greenville News, 21 June 1971, p. 13.
10 "Morgan Drives In Three Runs For Astros, 4-2." The Jacksonville Daily Journal, 24 June 1971, p. 26.
11 The Montgomery Advertiser, 26 June 1971, p. 10.
12 Astros Daily.

July

1   McCurdy, Bill. "July 2, 1971: Wynn Leads Astros to 3-2 Win." The Pecan Park Eagle, 13 Mar. 2014, bill37mccurdy.com/2014/03/13/july-2-1971-wynn-leads-astros-to-3-2-win/. Accessed 06 Apr. 2025.
2   "Baseball Tickets Going Fast." Corpus Christi Caller-Times, 24 June 1971, p. 67.
3   Maysel, Lou. "Astros' 18-4 Blast Draws Attention." Austin American-Statesman, 11 July 1971, p. 31.
4   Dierker, Larry. "Being An All Star." 49's Fastball Podcast, 26 July 2018.
5   Astros Daily.

6   Major League Baseball. 1971 All Star Game Official Ballot, 1971.
7   Jacobson, Steve. "It Wasn't Pure Rockne but It Worked." Newsday, 16 July 1971, p. 95.
8   Astros Daily.
9   Carmichael, John P. "Wynn Episode One Of Many 'Short Fuses' Ignited." Corpus Christi Times, 21 July 1971, p. 53.
10   "Astros' Wynn Threatens Houston Sports Writer." The Holland Evening Sentinel, 17 July 1971, p. 14.
11   Mack, Darrell. "Lucchesi Accuses Umps Of A No-No." The Press Democrat, 20 July 1971, p. 10.
12   "Portrait of Willie Mays (ABC, 1967)." YouTube, ABC, 2017, www.youtube.com/watch?v=zPSdJlthCBs&t=1273s. Accessed 30 May 2024.
13   "Morgan's Boot Costs Astros." Corpus Christi Times, 22 July 1971, p. 36.
14   Wynn. (Pg. 64)
15   Harner, A. (2024, July 31). July 26, 1971: Phillies' Mike Ryan shows 'great courage' by playing 15 innings after freak injury. Society for American Baseball Research. https://sabr.org/gamesproj/game/july-26-1971-phillies-mike-ryan-shows-great-courage-by-playing-15-innings-after-freak-injury/
16   "Marathon Win - - Astros Gain In West Division." The Baytown Sun, 27 July 1971, p. 9.
17   "Astros Down Phils 7-4." The Reporter, 27 July 1971, p. 13.
18   "Cubs Come to Dome Monday - - Astros In Do-Or-Die Homestand." The Baytown Sun, 1AD, p. 7.

August

1   "Cubs Come to Dome Monday - - Astros In Do-Or-Die Homestand."
2   Yellon, Al. "Today in Cubs History: The Time Leo Durocher Ripped a Phone off the Astrodome Dugout Wall." Bleed Cubbie Blue, 26 Aug. 2021, www.bleedcubbieblue.

com/2021/8/26/22642675/today-cubs-history-leo-durocher-ripped-phone-astrodome-dugout-wall. Accessed 02 June 2024.

3   "Houston Meets Cubs Monday." Longview News-Journal, 1 Aug. 1971, p. 10.

4   Bock, Hal. "Sacramento's Forsch Blanks LA." The Sacramento Bee, 5 Aug. 1971, p. 54.

5   Black, John. "Astros, Padres In Dome Tonight." The Baytown Sun, 6 Aug. 1971, p. 6.

6   Miller. (Pg. 151-151)

7   Black, John. "Astros, Padres Wrap Up Homestand." The Baytown Sun, 8AD, p. 8.

8   "Nickel Beer Night at the Astrodome Ends, Appropriately, with a Miller." This Day In Baseball, Promotions, 26 July 2022, thisdayinbaseball.com/1971-nickel-beer-night-at-the-dome-ends-appropriately-with-a-miller-bob-miller-of-san-diego-tosses-a-1-2-3-ninth-to-seal-a-4-3-houston-loss-after-the-game-drunken-fans-spill-onto-the-field/. Accessed 24 Apr. 2024.

9   "El Paso Girl Crowned Miss Astro." El Paso Times, 9 Aug. 1971, p. 20.

10   "Wynn Sees Likely Swap From Astros." The Times Recorder, 8AD, p. 9.

11   Lawson. "Wynn Denies Asking for Trade." The Cincinnati Post, 11 Aug. 1971, p. 29.

12   Black, John. "Dierker's Sore Arm Hinders Astro Hopes." The Baytown Sun, 9 Aug. 1971, p. 9.

13   Hertzel, Bob. "Nolan, Errors Traumatize Astros." The Cincinnati Enquirer, 12 Aug. 1971, p. 35.

14   Hudspeth, Ron. "Braves Rip Astros, 7-0, On Three-Hitter." The Atlanta Constitution, 15 Aug. 1971, p. 77.

15   "Wynn Wants To Start Helping The Astros." Pampa Daily News, 16 Aug. 1971, p. 8.

16   Magee, Chris. "Crisscrossing Sports." The Odessa American, 18 Aug. 1971, p. 19.

17 Black, John. "Houston Still Seeking First Win - - Astros, Cards, Set Series Finale." The Baytown Sun, 25 Aug. 1971, p. 16.

18 "Metzger Night Aug. 30." Austin-American Statesman, 22 Aug. 1971, p. 48.

19 Black, John. "Houston Still Seeking First Win - - Astros, Cards, Set Series Finale." The Baytown Sun, 25 Aug. 1971, p. 16.

20 "Astro Game Will Honor Old Timers." The Brookshire Times, 26 Aug. 1971, p. 7.

21 "Harry 'The Hat' Says 'Quit Bellyaching Astros.'" Tyler Morning Telegraph, 30 Aug. 1971, p. 10.

22 "Metzger Night Aug. 30."

23 "Astros End Worst Stand At Home In Club History." The Kilgore News Herald, 2 Sept. 1971, p. 5.

24 "Ex-Astro Stars." The Daily Republic, 1 Sept. 1971, p. 14.

September

1 "Astros Get Needed Help From 89ers." *The Baytown Sun*, 2 Sept. 1971, p. 8.

2 Stellino, Vito. "Buckner, Lefebvre Dance; Cedeno Romps. Dodger Tangle Tango Out Of Step With Astro Beat." The Californian, 3AD, p. 18.

3 "Grand Slam Rarity 'Cheap' - Walter Alston." Fort Lauderdale News, 3AD, p. 28.

4 Griffin, Tom, and Samuel Barrett. "Phone Call W/ Tom Griffin." 27 Nov. 2024.

5 Kane, Tom. "McCovey Is Injured As Astros Beat Giants Twice." The Sacramento Bee, 6 Sept. 1971, p. 29.

6 Dierker, Larry. "Dierk's Dugout Reflections." 2015.

7 Culver, George, and Samuel Barrett. "Phone Call W/ George Culver, Part 2." 26 Oct. 2024

8 "Spinks, Busse Spark Astros' Rookie Parade." The Columbus Ledger, 7 Sept. 1971, p. 18.

9   Ramsey, Mike. "Rambling Around." The Orange Leader, 7 Sept. 1971, p. 7.

10   "Harry 'The Hat"s Last Season." The Waco Citizen, 9AD, p. 6.

11   Wynn. (Pg. 108)

12   Ferguson, Jim. "Astro Blasts Two Homers. Mayberry Delivers Reds To The Grave, 5-2." Dayton Daily News, 12AD, p. 66.

13   "Wes Parker Is Happy." Progress Bulliten, 1 Sept. 1971, p. 33.

14   "Astros' Rader Has Operation." Johnson City Press, 17 Sept. 1971, p. 15.

15   "Rader To Enter Hospital Today." The Waxahachie Daily Light, 14 Sept. 1971, p. 4.

16   Black, John. "Surging Houston Seeks 9th Straight Win - - Astros, Padres In Dome Again Tonight." The Baytown Sun, 14 Sept. 1971, p. 4.

17   Pomrenke, Jacob. "September 15, 1971: Larry Yount Makes His Big-League Debut, and Farewell, for Astros." *Society for American Baseball Research*, Jacob Pomrenke /Wp-Content/ Uploads/2020/02/Sabr_logo.Png, 13 July 2020, sabr.org/gamesproj/game/september-15-1971-larry-yount-makes-his-big-league-debut-and-farewell-for-astros/. Accessed 09 June 2025.

18   Astros Daily.

19   Mack, Darrell. "Being HR Leader Not Good - Joe." The Town Talk, 20 Sept. 1971, p. 10.

20   "Astros Begrudge Giants: Marichal." The Times, 23 Sept. 1971, p. 21.

21   "Giants Beat Astros, Boost Lead To Three." The Spokesman-Review, 25 Sept. 1971, p. 17.

22   "Mantle Wants To Manage Transplanted Senators." The San Bernadino County Sun, 24 Sept. 1971, p. 11.

23   "Move Over Astros, Make Way For Senators / Spec Feels Sens Won't Hurt Astros." The Brownsville Herald, 22 Sept. 1971, p. 21.

24   Spinks, Scipio, and Samuel Barrett.

25 Culver, George, and Samuel Barrett. "Phone Call W/ George Culver, Part 1."

26 "Padres, Astros Split Double." The Sun Times, 25 Sept. 1971, p. 12.

27 "They Played All Night." The Cincinnati Post, 25 Sept. 1971, p. 12.

28 Spinks, Scipio, and Samuel Barrett.

29 Lutz, Michael A. "Judge Rehires Hat and Spec." Del Rio News Herald, 27 Sept. 1971, p. 6.

30 Lutz, Michael A. "Astros Will Wear Same 'Hat' In 1972." The Shreveport Journal, 28 Sept. 1971, p. 6.

October

1 "What National League Managers Are Saying; Schoendienst Figures Pirates Team to Beat in N.L. East." The Sunday News and Tribune, 4 Apr. 1971, p. 15.

2 Wynn. (Pg. 132)

3 Dierker, Larry. "Being An All Star." 49's Fastball Podcast, 26 July 2018.

4 Bike, William S. Received by Samuel Barrett, Baseball Books, 14 May 2024.

5 "Pythagorean Winning Percentage | Glossary." MLB.com, www.mlb.com/glossary/advanced-stats/pythagorean-winning-percentage.

What Could Have Been: The Team

1 Smith, Tal, and Samuel Barrett, #1.

2 Smith, Tal, and Samuel Barrett, #2.

3 Wynn. (Pg. 66)

4 Brown. (Pg. 20)

5 Houston Astros Official Program and Scorecard, 1971. (Pg. 53)

6 Pittman, Darrell. "The All-Rookie Game." AstrosDaily.Com, www.astrosdaily.com/history/19630927/index.html#:~:text=Two%20days%20before%20the%20end,MLB's%20youngest%2Dever%20starting%20lineup. Accessed 03 Apr. 2025.

7   Treder, Steve. "The Virtual 1972 Houston Astros (Part 1)." The Hardball Times, 3 Oct. 2008, tht.fangraphs.com/the-virtual-1972-houston-astros-part-1/. Accessed 27 Dec. 2024.

8   Morgan. (Pg. 104-105)

9.   Wynn. (Pg. 106)

10   Dierker, Larry. *This Ain't Brain Surgery: How to Win The Pennant Without Losing Your Mind.* (Pg. 212)

11   Barrett, Samuel, and Larry Dierker.

12   Watson. (Pg. 96)

13   Luksa, Frank. "Fool-Proof Plan To Pep Up Astros." Fort Worth Star-Telegram, 5 June 1971, p. 21.

14   Vance, Mike, and Samuel Barrett.

15   "Astros Memories: The Greatest Moments in Astros Baseball History." Major League Baseball Productions, 2013.

16   "Extended Interview with Aaron Pointer." YouTube, KING 5 Seattle, 22 Feb. 2023, www.youtube.com/watch?v=ZweMaDIKBx-U&t=737s. Accessed 29 Mar. 2024.

17   Lauck, John. "The Astros All-Time Team - Rotation." AstrosDaily. Com, www.astrosdaily.com/history/alltime/rotation.html. Accessed 18 June 2025.

18   Spinks, Scipio, and Samuel Barrett.

19   Corbett, Warren. "Mike Marshall." Society for American Baseball Research, admin /wp-content/uploads/2020/02/sabr_logo.png, 4 Apr. 2022, sabr.org/bioproj/person/mike-marshall/.

20   DeFillipo, Larry. "Mel McGaha." Society for American Baseball Research, 2 July 2023, sabr.org/bioproj/person/mel-mcgaha/. Accessed 16 June 2024.

21   Morgan. (Pg. 112)

22   Miller, Norm, and Samuel Barrett. "Phone Call W/ Norm Miller." 30 Sept. 2024.

23   Morgan. (Pg. 111)

24 Ross, Ken. "Admin." Society for American Baseball Research, Admin /Wp-Content/Uploads/2020/02/Sabr_logo.Png, 24 Sept. 2021, sabr.org/bioproj/person/hub-kittle/. Accessed 13 Feb. 2025.

25 Dierker, Larry. *This Ain't Brain Surgery: How to Win The Pennant Without Losing Your Mind.* (Pg. 211)

The 1971 Houston Astros

1 *1968 Major League Baseball All Star Game.* NBC, 9 July 1968.

2 Flaherty, Will. "The Houston Astros and Wooing Women Fans." Society for American Baseball Research, The National Pastime: Baseball in the Space Age (Houston, 2014), 25 Oct. 2021, sabr. org/journal/article/the-houston-astros-and-wooing-women-fans/.

3 Swoboda, Ron. Here's The Catch: A Memoir of the Miracle Mets and More. St. Martin's Press, 2021.

4 49's Fastball Podcast. Houston Astrodome Scoreboard, Larry Dierker, Houston, Texas, 6 Feb. 2018.

5 "Astros Memories: The Greatest Moments in Astros Baseball History."

6 Miller. (Pg. 64)

7 Barrett, Samuel. "Questions to Norm Miller." Received from Norm Miller, 17 Jan. 2023.

8 Czerwinski, Kevin. "Here Comes The Rooster." BallNine, 19 Sept. 2021, ballnine.com/2021/09/17/here-comes-the-rooster/. Accessed 18 Nov. 2023.

9 Nowlin.

10 Wynn. (Pg. 60)

11 Pryor, Fred, and Gary Livacari. Paul Pryor in His Own Words: The Life and Times of a 20-Year Major League Umpire. Amazon Direct Publishing Platform, 2018. (Pg. 66)

Houston Astros Official Program and Scorecard, 1971.

ABOUT THE AUTHOR

S amuel Barrett, 24, has worn numerous hats in the baseball realm. He played high school baseball in his senior year of 2019 at Central High School in Phenix City, AL. He began an ongoing career as an umpire in 2021 when he attended the Wendelstedt Umpire School, from which he earned his first league placement and was spurred to begin calling high school games in Alabama as well as college-level games for three years. Barrett's story through his first  year as an umpire is told in his first book *Umpire Diary: My Personal Journey and Experiences Beginning an Umpire Career*, which was published in July 2024. He joined the brand-new Columbus Clingstones, double-A affiliate of the Atlanta Braves, as a pitch clock operator in 2025. Barrett first began watching the Astros in 2015 since his father's lineage originates in south Texas, and soon started researching baseball history, including Astros history, which eventually developed into the inspiration for this book. He is grateful for the opportunities he has created and received, especially given his status on the autism spectrum, which thanks to proactive early intervention at a time before Barrett can remember, is now not noticeable without being told so. He is humbled and honored that you, the reader, believe his work to be worthy of your time reading it, and he can be reached at rsbarrett00@gmail.com.

www.ingramcontent.com/pod-product-compliance
Lightning Source LLC
Chambersburg PA
CBHW051614120626
46551CB00014B/1786